Life in Death: A Journey From Terrorism to Triumph

By Lisa Gibson

xulon
PRESS

What people are saying about "Life in Death: A Journey from Terrorism to Triumph"

"Lisa Gibson, an attorney, is the Executive Director of the *Peace and Prosperity Alliance*, a remarkable pioneering charity on behalf of Libya. She has a deep authentic calling to be ambassador of reconciliation. Engulfed by terrorism herself, she has been through the fires, and emerged as gold. To reflectively read this book is to go farther in coming to terms with what God truly wants to see in Christians loving their enemies. Gibson takes it from religious poetry to teeth gritting reality. How I yearn that every Western Christian who is repulsed by Muslim terrorism would follow in her steps."
Dr. Greg Livingstone
Founder of *Frontiers*

"My favorite story is how, against all expectations, Christ redeems us and moves us to thoroughly and deeply love even our enemies. This is Lisa's life and passion. Few of us boldly embrace the pain and joy of crossing the chasm which divides our world while living out, as Lisa has, the full repercussions of Christ's amazing intervention. She encouraged me to be bold and run into the wind."
Keith Swartley, Editor of *Encountering the World of Islam*

"To most of us the downing of Pan Am Flight 103 over Lockerbie Scotland on December 21, 1988 was another news story. To Lisa Gibson it was far more.

For that was the day when her brother Ken, who she dearly loved, stepped into eternity. This is her loving response to her brother's tragic death at the hands of Muslim extremists, and her amazing ministry to which it gave birth. Every American needs to read this book."
Eddie Smith, Author and Speaker
www.usprayercenter.org

"This is a remarkable story of one woman's struggle with tragedy and her care for those who many would say are her enemies."
Congressman Joseph R. Pitts

"*Life in Death* contains the powerful message of how to move from great tragedy into the triumph of a Christian walk truly surrendered to the cross of Jesus and His love. Lisa brilliantly teaches the principles of how to forgive and love in the terrible throes of Islamic terrorism. Learn through her personal journey how to forgive and love your enemies and to move beyond hurt into victory. This inspiring book contains price-less treasures from the word of God that will challenge and encourage all readers to search their hearts and embrace the love of God for all humanity and to seek and pursue God for His purpose and calling in their lives. Thank you, Lisa, for this great message."
Rebecca Greenwood
President and Co-Founder, *Christian Harvest International*

Dedication:

To my brother, Kenneth J. Gibson, and the countless other innocent people who have lost their lives at the hands of terrorist. May God's love overtake the hate that motivates these attacks and may all those that have been affected find healing and restoration.

Acknowledgements

I am indebted to those friends and colleagues who offered suggestions, contributed biblical insights, and prayed for me and this project. I especially want to thank Karen Martello, Anne Cumming Rice, Gayle Ann Perry, Catherine M. Thompson, Heidi Feenstra, Cynthia Alderman, and Rilla Giesick, for their input, encouragement, and support during the process of writing the book. To my parents, Ruth and Larry Gibson, for their love, understanding, and support of my desire to write this book.

Table of Contents

Introduction

"The Lord is with me; he is my helper. I will look in triumph on my enemies." – Psalm 118:7 NIV

Today we are at war! Militant Muslims continue to wage a war of hate and fear through terrorist plots to destroy countries like ours. Years before the tragedy of September 11, 2001, the words "war on terror" were already deeply burned into my mind and heart. For nearly 20 years, I have been learning what it is to use the pain and anguish of losing a loved one to terrorism to effectively engage in the battle against the evil of terrorism. We can no longer be naïve to the threat to our sense of well-being or the very beliefs we hold dear.

This book is about the loss of my brother in the terrorist bombing of Pan Am flight 103 over Lockerbie, Scotland on December 21, 1988. It was the worst terrorist attack against U.S. citizens prior to September 11, 2001. It is a story that has been 20 years in the making, about how God can use even the most evil act of hate and turn it around for His redemptive purposes. It is a book for anyone that has experienced the sudden death of a loved one, who finds himself struggling with the question "why?" But more importantly, it is for every person who struggles with the fear of the imminent threat of Islamic terrorism that seems to be pressing in. It is a threat that is real, that we can no longer ignore. This book will especially resonate with Christians who find themselves in conflict over what the Bible teaches about "loving their enemies," yet find themselves bound in fear from interacting with the very people they are called to love.

We are engaged in a complex battle. The enemy of our souls seeks to steal and destroy everyone and everything that belongs to the Kingdom of God. We know that the battle we wage is against principalities and spiritual forces in the heavenly realms. Yet, Satan and his minions use deception to enlist the help of men and women around the world to carry out his destructive purposes. How do we effectively engage in the battle without falling victim to waging the battle with the enemy's weapons of fear and hate against the Muslim people? What examples can we gain from the way Christ lived His life and reached out to the very people who hated Him?

This is not a book about pat answers and easy solutions. Instead, it is a book about heart-wrenching pain and anguish, the lessons I have learned in the journey, and the doors that have opened to serve the very people that caused my pain. Through my brother's death, I had a choice — I could succumb to withholding forgiveness and grow bitter, or I could die to my selfish desires and allow God to transform death to life through His redemptive purposes. It is truly a love story of how God took a horrific act of evil against someone I dearly loved, and turned it around for God's glory. That glory is the only thing that could make my brother's death not be in vain.

My hope is that my story will encourage you to not shrink back in fear when the enemy attacks, but to learn to wage the war more effectively by fighting the enemy with the only effective weapon in this battle — the weapon of love.

"For every thousand hacking at the leaves of evil, there is one striking at the root." — Henry David Thoreau

Chapter 1 — The Tragedy

"Even though I walk through the valley of the shadow of death, I will fear no evil, for you are with me; your rod and your staff, they comfort me." — Psalms 23:4NLT

My heart was full of hopeful anticipation as I awoke on December 21, 1988. My entire family was eagerly awaiting my brother Ken's arrival. It had been nearly two years since we had last seen him, before he left for Germany to serve in the U.S. Army. Light snow covered the ground that Wednesday, the first day of winter in Romulus, Michigan.

The night before, I had difficulty falling asleep. I was restless with thousands of questions running through my mind. Would Ken look different? What kind of adventures had he experienced living in a foreign country? Who was this German girl he was dating? I prayed for him, his travels and for our time

17

together. I wanted the time with him to be peaceful and joyous, which was not always the case growing up in my family. Tensions were often high when Dad and Ken got together, because they didn't always see eye-to-eye.

As I prayed, I saw a picture of a plane in my mind's eye and a flash of light like an explosion. I was shaken.

Not having any knowledge at the time that such images can be prophetic, I passed off the image as a figment of my imagination. The last thing I wanted to do was to somehow "jinx" things by thinking of such an image. So I quickly pushed the thought aside before drifting off to sleep.

That Wednesday Ken was supposed to arrive for Christmas, there wasn't much on the agenda. Ken's flight wasn't scheduled to arrive into Detroit Metropolitan Airport until around 4 p.m. So, I used the opportunity to catch up on my rest a bit by sleeping in until almost 10 a.m. Wiping the sleep from my eyes, and any remnant of that disturbing picture from the night before, I rolled out of bed and headed down to the kitchen for some breakfast. My mother was off work that day and busy with last-minute house cleaning and preparations to make her delectable pot of spaghetti, one of Ken's favorite meals. My dad had left for work early that morning, while my two younger brothers went off to junior high and high school. I got my customary bowl of Cheerios and nestled onto the couch to watch some television.

Growing Up With Ken

I had just finished the fall semester of my freshman year at Alma College in Alma, Michigan. With Christmas only four days away, a festive spirit was in the air. I had gotten all A's and B's my first semester, had an enjoyable first season on the college volleyball team, and was smitten with Todd, a junior member of the swim team, whom I had been dating for three months. *What could be better?* I was anxious to see Ken and share with him all that had been happening in my life.

Like most sibling relationships, my relationship with Ken had included the characteristic fights and bad attitudes at times. There were four kids in our family. Ken was the eldest, and I was born two years after him. Two younger brothers, Eric and Jason, came along four and six years later. We had some tough seasons, such as during my freshman year in high school when Ken was retaking freshman civics because he failed it the first time. Our class seats were organized alphabetically, so Ken was assigned to sit directly behind me during class. No one would have ever suspected that we were related, because he forbade me from telling anyone and refused to talk with me. But things had changed over the years while he was in Germany. We were both growing up and putting aside our childish ways. I no longer saw Ken as the same unmotivated and angry young man I grew up with. I had gained a new respect and admiration for him as my older and much more experienced brother. After all, he was living in a foreign land and experiencing all kinds of new adventures, things I greatly desired to do. Plus, he was faithfully serving his country in the Army. It seemed that he was finally finding something to soothe his restless soul and to motivate him to succeed. I was incredibly proud of him. I was also anxious to introduce him to my boyfriend, Todd, and to just catch up on the details that we hadn't had the chance to share in the years that we had been apart.

A specialist in the U.S. Army Infantry division, Ken had been serving his country as part of the Berlin Brigade in Berlin, Germany, for nearly two years. The Berlin Brigade was assigned to monitor and protect U.S. interests in the area near the Berlin Wall, which divided East and West Germany at the time, about two years prior to the fall of the Berlin Wall and the dissolution of communism in the former Soviet Union.

Before being called up to serve in Germany, Ken went through boot camp at Camp Benning, Georgia. After dropping out of high school during his senior year, he bounced around among menial jobs. After taking his GED exam, he had two choices: go to community college or join the military. Ken tried one term at community college and despite his high intelligence level, he knew that he lacked the motivation needed to succeed. So within a month, he had committed to serve four years in the Army.

While Ken was away, we had become accustomed to writing periodically. Money was tight, phone calls were expensive, and with so many soldiers sharing the limited number of telephones in the barracks, regular phone conversations were not possible. The occasional phone calls were always brief, so that everyone in the family could get a chance to talk with him. I always had so much more I wanted to share, but it just was never possible. So, I loved getting Ken's letters to our family and was always the first one to write him back. I found that writing letters to him was somewhat of a therapeutic exercise for me, as I was navigating the transition from high school to college. It was my alternative to journal writing, because I could ask Ken advice about life and share more vulnerably with him about things I was feeling that I would have never even considered sharing in person. Somehow, the miles and distance between us created an invisible shield that prevented any kind of reproach from him, which would have been common when we were younger.

In our letters, there was never the usual antagonistic banter or competitive spirit that was ever present during our childhood years. Something had drastically changed. Ken was genuinely proud of me, and I of him. It was truly a sweet time in our relationship, and I yearned to spend time with him and reconnect.

First Reports

Just before noon, the Wednesday that Ken was supposed to arrive home, my mother got a call from her longtime childhood friend, Olivia. "What time is Ken supposed to get in?" Olivia asked.

"Around 4 p.m.," my mother said. "I don't know the specifics, but he plans to call when he arrives at the airport. Why?"

"Oh, no reason," she responded.

Since our family lived only five minutes from the airport, my parents didn't even think twice about the fact that Ken hadn't given them a flight itinerary. We only knew that he was coming from Berlin and the approximate time his plane was supposed to arrive. Mom hung up the phone and went back to preparing the spaghetti. Within an hour, the phone rang again. This time it was a woman from Mom's work, named Patty Cooper. It was strange for Patty to call Mom during the workday from the office.

"What time is Ken coming in and what flight is he on?" Patty asked.

"Why are you wondering all this?" Mom responded, starting to believe something was wrong.

Patty explained that her husband had called her at work, saying he had seen a news story on television about a plane that had crashed in the British Isles. But Patty tried to reassure Mom that Ken probably wasn't on that plane.

By this point, Mom was beginning to get curious. She got off the phone and came into the living room, where I was watching television.

These were the days before 24-hour news coverage on the Internet or television networks like CNN, so we were at the mercy of local and national network news to get word of what was happening in the world.

There were periodic interruptions of regular programs for special reports on the plane crash. When the noon hour arrived, I flipped through the stations until I found a news show. The lead story was about a plane that had gone down over a small town in Scotland called Lockerbie, but details at that point were still pretty hazy. Everyone on board had been killed.

We continued to watch as the details unfolded. Our hearts began to sink for everyone involved. Mom started to toy with the idea that Ken might be on board, but felt pretty secure that he couldn't have been on the plane because he was coming from Berlin. It was a Pan American jumbo jet bound from London to New York that had crashed into Lockerbie. The Boeing 747 slammed into a gasoline station and a row of houses in the small town of 2,500 residents, 15 miles north of the English border, igniting a fire-ball that rose 300 feet into the sky. The fuselage of the plane left a crater in the ground approximately 20 feet deep and 100 feet long.

Mom tried to do the math in her head to figure out the probability with flight time and distance, to determine if Ken could have been on board. *He would have had to have been on an earlier flight to be here by 4 p.m.,* Mom thought. We sat there glued to the television as we waited, praying silently for the families of those affected.

Then the news reported that the plane had been on a layover at Heathrow Airport in London. The plane had left Heathrow at 6:25 p.m. local time, and the last contact from the crew was at 7:15 p.m., when the plane was cruising at 31,000 feet. Flight 103 originated in Frankfurt as a Boeing 727 and changed to a 747 at Heathrow, where additional passengers boarded.

The plane was only half-full with 243 passengers and a crew of 15, and it was scheduled to land at New York's John F. Kennedy International Airport at 9:19 p.m. The flight was to end in Detroit.

Confusion And Denial

Numb to what I was seeing, I sat on the couch, dazed with confusion. All I could think of was the vision the night before. *Oh, please, no God!* I was overcome with guilt. *Please God, no, I will do anything you ask me if you please make this not true.* The news reported that, as rescue teams reached the crash scene, there were indications of an explosion aboard the plane. The jet's cabin door was found about 10 miles from the rest of the cockpit, while an engine was found on a highway outside town. The one intact piece of the aircraft to fall to the ground was the nose cone, flight deck and forward part of the first class cabin, which was ripped off from the rest of the fuselage by the force of the explosion.

We waited for more details, vacillating between concern for the victims' family members and worry about the possibility of Ken being on the plane.

Our small townhouse was located directly across the street from Detroit Metropolitan Airport. We had grown accustomed to the sound of planes flying low over our home as they were coming in for landing. But today was different. *I wonder if that's Ken's flight.* Each plane that flew over drew my attention like it never had before. These were the days before cell phones, so there was no one to call. We simply sat idly with our eyes fixed to the television and waited.

The 4 o'clock hour came and went, and we heard nothing from Ken. Mom paced the floors nervously. Eric and Jason had gotten home from school and we all sat anxiously awaiting any updates that might be forthcoming on the 5 o'clock news. Any hope that we had previously clung to was quickly eroding away.

My mother broke down in tears. "Oh, no, please no!" she cried. "It can't be."

Around 5:30 p.m. my father came home from work. Mom told him about the news that we had so far, including the phone calls she had received, the news of the crash, and that Ken had not called for her to come and pick him up.

This was the first time Dad heard of the tragedy. In his typical take-charge fashion, he grabbed the phone and dialed Pan Am Airlines. He paced back and forth while waiting, hoping to reach a human being. When Dad finally got through to a customer service representative, she simply confirmed that Ken was listed on the flight manifest.

We all huddled around the phone, waiting for the answer.

"Oh my God, he was on the plane," Dad said before breaking down in tears. My mom and two younger brothers started weeping as well.

But I remained unemotional, unwilling to believe Ken had been on the plane. "Maybe they're wrong," I said.

Dad immediately called the airlines back to get more details. Somewhere within that five-minute timeframe, airline officials pulled the manifest and prohibited the agents from confirming who was and wasn't on board the flight. The next customer service representative refused to release any details, including whether Ken was even on the flight.

Dad became furious. "They just told me my son was on that plane," he yelled into the phone.

"Official notification has to come from an official Pan Am Airlines representative," the agent said.

This threw us into confusion. *Was Ken on the plane or not?* I calmly held out hope, while the rest of my family gave into a myriad of emotions, from anger to grief. That moment felt like an out-of-body experience to me, as if I was watching a movie, not living out a nightmare come true.

Maybe he just missed his flight. Maybe he's safe but can't get to a phone to call us. I'm sure he's fine. I conjured up this image in my mind of Ken wandering the streets of Germany, looking for a way to get in touch with us.

When faced with trauma, the mind has the incredible ability to create alternate scenarios. My natural tendency was to deny bad things until I was forced to deal with the reality. I had learned through the years to compartmentalize bad or uncomfortable things, and this situation was no different.

This scenario would not seem plausible to a rational mind, but when faced with trauma, you will believe almost anything before the truth. Until I knew with absolute certainty that Ken was on that plane, I would not fully believe it.

Chapter 2 — Our Fears Are Confirmed

"Fear and trembling come upon me, and horror overwhelms me." – Psalm 55:5 NLT

As the evening unfolded, Dad called the airport nine or ten times, trying to get information, to no avail. As time wore on and we had not heard from Ken, we started to ponder the possibility that maybe Ken was on that plane and that it had not been a mistake.

At 8:30 p.m., Dad called Grandma Frances to give her the news we had so far. Ken had a very close relationship with her. She and Grandpa Jack were my Dad's parents. Our grandparents on my Mom's side had passed away years before. During Ken's first couple years of life, my parents lived with Grandma Frances and Grandpa Jack, so my grandparents became quite bonded and attached to Ken. We had planned to spend a family Christmas with

Grandma and Grandpa in the northern Michigan town of Onaway, where they lived. A six-hour drive prevented them from being with us in person, so Grandma called her sister Amy to come over to be with our family and support us.

Dad made phone calls to anyone and everyone he could think of who might be able to provide answers, including the top brass Army leadership in Germany. The rest of us just carried on a vigil, hoping and praying that our fears were not confirmed. Aunt Amy tried to encourage us to keep our hopes up, but Mom was already moving toward accepting the inevitable.

Around midnight, we received the official news from the Pan Am 103 representative. Ken had been on the flight.

Mom was surprisingly calm, trying to figure out how to respond. But Dad needed more answers. "Can you confirm whether my son Ken was wearing his military uniform?" he asked the airline representative, thinking that would confirm whether Ken was, indeed, on the plane.

"Your son was in the military?" she said. "Oh my, I wasn't supposed to notify you. I am so sorry. The military is required to notify military family members in person."

Despite having our worst fears confirmed, we were glad the representative called because we didn't receive the official news from the military until mid-afternoon the following day.

That night I didn't sleep much. I was thoroughly exhausted from all that had transpired that day, but

I was restless. My mind played back all the images that I had seen that day. It was like a film reel that was on a continual loop, showing the same pictures again and again — the images of the plane wreckage, the sirens blaring and ambulances flying down streets of that small Scottish town, the fire burning the buildings in Lockerbie, and the horrified looks on the faces of the first responders and law enforcement as they released the details of the tragedy.

I wanted to pinch myself to see if it was a real. It was a horrific dream that I desperately wanted to wake up from, but try as I might, I just couldn't shake the depths of it. As I remembered the vision from the night before, my heart sank with guilt. *Did I cause this? Where is God in all of this?*

I felt very alone.

News From The Military

The following day was a blur of confusion as Mom and I navigated the continual onslaught of calls from family, friends, and the media. Mom and I were home alone. My younger brothers went to school — my parents thought it was a bad idea, but Eric and Jason wanted to be with their friends in the midst of the tragedy, so they let them go. Dad, meanwhile, went to the airport to try to get more answers from Pan Am Airlines.

As I shared the story with people who called, I felt very distant from the plot, like an author telling a story from the third-person perspective. But the interruptions were welcome and helped to fill the space in the day, while providing an outlet for processing the tragedy itself.

That afternoon, we received the official military notification when a major and chaplain from the U.S. Army came to deliver the news. The knock came at the door and our hearts dropped. I looked through the peephole of the front door. "It's them," I said. I opened the door, and there stood two men in military uniforms.

"No, no, no!" Mom cried out as she shrunk back. Somehow, she believed that if the military hadn't come, it wasn't real. They read us a letter from an Army general, who confirmed that Specialist Kenneth J. Gibson was on the Pan Am flight 103 that was blown up over Lockerbie, Scotland at 19:03 hours. There were believed to be no survivors.

I sat there, perplexed, as the major tried to share any of the details that he could, and to offer any support or comfort to our family that the U.S. Army had at its disposal. Mom was bawling uncontrollably, and I sat there next to her and tried to comfort her. They informed us of the options for the funeral and Mom assured them that she wanted a full military funeral with everything Ken was eligible for. Both men were nice and caring, and I thought how difficult it must have been for them to have to deliver the news.

Ken's death still wasn't real to me. I thought I needed to be strong for my mother and brothers, so I set aside my own thoughts and feelings to support them. At the time, I didn't realize it, but I was in deep denial. For as long as I could remember, I had been the strong one in the family. When everyone else seemed to be melting down, I was able to step up and handle details. This was my role, or so I thought. I set my mind on continuing to press forward.

The news that day reported that several U.S. embassies in Europe had received telephone warnings about a Pan Am flight to the United States from Frankfurt. At the airport, talking to Pan Am officials, Dad was the first Lockerbie family member to ask why the airlines hadn't done anything about the warnings, or at least informed people so they could make a choice whether or not to fly. Quickly, the news media got wind of it, and that evening he was interviewed on "Nightline."

Many tough questions were beginning to be asked and would continue to be asked as the controversy unfolded.

Media Attention

Like most people, I had dreams of one day being important enough to be a celebrity or featured on television. In my imagination, I thought it would come about through being a model or movie star, and not because my life was thrust into the public view by a tragedy. There is no guidebook or seminar on how to navigate the shrewd reporters and overwhelming media attention that tragedies bring. Our family was a simple family of modest means, that suddenly found our faces on the front page of the newspaper in one of the most highly profiled tragedies of the decade.

Prior to the World Trade Center terrorist attacks on September 11, 2001, the bombing of Pan Am flight

103 over Lockerbie, Scotland, was the single worst terrorist attack against Americans. A combination of airport delay and high winds caused the disaster to occur over Lockerbie, rather than the open sea. When all the fire and smoke cleared, all 259 on board and 11 people on the ground were dead. *How could and should our family respond – not just from a human perspective, but from a Christian perspective?* These were the questions I was asking myself. We believed it was an intentional act of terrorism, but we still had no idea who was responsible.

After Dad did the interview for "Nightline," we did interviews for all the major media networks. I learned very quickly that some reporters are not in the business of just reporting the facts. Instead, they have an agenda that includes twisting or sensationalizing details in order to make things more intriguing or newsworthy. When hearing news that my brother's remains had been found, one reporter had the audacity to ask what kind of remains had been found. Mom was aghast. She let him know what an insensitive jerk he was. Of course, when you lose a loved one in a plane explosion at 30,000 feet, that question runs through your head, but in your heart that is the last thing you want to know the answer to.

As a young woman of only 18, I had not been prepared for what I would encounter while interviewing with the media. Some of the reporters we interviewed with seemed compassionate and sensitive to our situation. But others were like a pit of vipers desperate for kill. I am sure they were looking for an Emmy Award-winning story or promotion. I naively thought being interviewed would be an opportunity to share a bit about my brother Ken and his story, and our family's perspective as Christians who had suffered from this tragedy. As a pre-law major, I had already been conditioned to believe in the importance of justice. As a follower of Christ, I knew we served a just God. As such, God would support our seeking justice against the person responsible for the Lockerbie bombing. That is a much different posture than revenge. I also knew that as God is just, He is also merciful and forgiving. So, my challenge was to figure out how to walk-out all those principles in my brother's death.

Our family did back-to-back interviews with ABC, NBC and CBS news. One news reporter from a Detroit station started out with a tone that led me to believe that he was looking to elicit information from my mother and me, which might not be consistent with how we actually felt. Since the interview was scheduled for live airing on the 5 o'clock news, I realized that what we said would be conveyed in its entirety. Despite my inexperience, I knew that I was not going to share anything I wasn't comfortable sharing. When my time came to be questioned, he asked a few introductory questions about my brother Ken. Then came the curve ball.

"So, you want revenge, don't you?" he asked.

"No, I want justice," I said.

Then he asked me a few follow-up questions, where he continued to try to twist my comments to get me to say I wanted revenge. Following the interview, I was quite disturbed with his interview tactics. As a Christian, I knew that revenge was wrong. Of course that wasn't what I wanted. But to my dismay, that evening on the 11 o'clock news, an edited version of my interview was re-aired with the reporter introducing the story by saying, "A sister in Romulus wants revenge."

I was outraged. "What? That is not what I said. How can he get away with that?"

My mother was flabbergasted as well. "Now the whole world is going to think I want revenge," I lamented. The fire of anger welled up within me. I was crushed, angered, and disillusioned. I couldn't bear the thought of people seeing me as a vengeful person. I was still very confused as to the depth of what was in my heart, but I did want to respond righteously, I knew that. *At least God knew my true heart. He's most important.*

A couple weeks after the bombing, Dad finally reached his limit with the media. We had been forthcoming for quite a while. But enough was enough. A reporter called wanting more information for a story. Dad simply said this: "You have used us for news and we have used the media to get our message of 'why weren't the passengers informed' out. Now we are done." Then he politely ended the conversation. That was Dad's last conversation with the media about the Lockerbie bombing.

Christmas Time

The hottest topic in the news that Christmas season was that the plane over Lockerbie was blown up by an explosive device, and it was believed to be an act of terrorism. The crash debris suggested the bomb was made of a high-performance plastic explosive. Calls began to flood in from close friends and family and long-time acquaintances. Needless to say, it was very overwhelming. Everyone wanted to help or just to offer condolences. But what can you say? None of it made any sense and there were still very few answers.

The final days leading up to and through Christmas were a fog. Because it was Christmas break, we were sheltered from regular contact with our friends at school. In an effort to try to return to life as usual, I decided to go through with attending my boyfriend Todd's parents' Christmas party on December 23rd. What should have been a joyous time was dulled by the circumstances I found myself in. I was completely numb to the whole experience and unable to appreciate the depth and breadth of it.

We decided to go ahead with plans to travel to my Grandma and Grandpa's house for Christmas, as we had originally planned. Perhaps we would be able to salvage some semblance of a holiday spirit together, or at a minimum be there to comfort one another. So early on Christmas Eve morning, we packed up the vehicle and drove six hours to Grandma's house. As was typical, Mom and Dad had waited until the last minute to do Christmas shopping. But the ensuing chaos of the days preceding Christmas prevented that. So on Christmas Eve, they went to store to find some last minute gifts for Eric, Jason, and me.

I loved being at Grandma's house that Christmas. I had always had a close relationship with Grandma, and being at her house always felt more like home than any other place ever had. The peace and quiet of the country and the fresh air helped me think. But on that trip, I wasn't thinking about much of anything. I really wasn't processing what had happened, but merely soaking in the safety I felt being there. Everyone seemed to need to talk about Ken — remembering fun memories, what he was like as a child, and discussing the details of the bombing that we knew so far. Even though I wasn't ready to embrace the reality of it, I enjoyed hearing them share about Ken as I found refuge by busying myself with helping make meals for the family. Part of me wanted to escape from the reality that was pressing in, but I could think of no place that I would rather escape to than Grandma's house.

On Christmas Day, details about the bombing continued to unfold. On the day that Christians everywhere celebrated Jesus' birth, we simply mourned Ken's death. We opened presents like we normally would. But how could we feel joy? Ken was supposed to be with us on that special day. It had been nearly two years since we had seen him, and we had so longed for him to be there with us.

My parents were coming to terms with the fact that Christmas would never again be the same, and they would never again see their son. For all of the Pan Am 103 families, the Christmas season has continued to be a constant reminder of the loss of something very dear to us — not a loss that is simply an accident, or a natural course in a person's journey through life, but a crime directed at innocent people in a senseless act of terrorism.

An Unlikely Community

A couple days after Christmas, my family was invited to participate in a candlelight ceremony in memory of the victims of Pan Am 103, with the Lockerbie family members from the Detroit area. None of us had received word on when our loved ones' bodies would be returned for burial, so this was the best we could do to have a corporate gathering in memory of those who were killed.

The ceremony was held at the home church of one of the men killed on the plane. It was our family's first connection with the other victims' families. We were complete strangers from many different walks of life, whose paths would never have crossed had it not been for our common loss. In spite of the heartache and pain wrought by the bombing, bereavement produced a unique bond between the victims' families and the people of Lockerbie. The victims from the Detroit area included James Fuller, senior vice president of Volkswagen of America, and their director of marketing, Lou Morengo; several members of the military; and a young Lebanese American named Khaled Jaafar of Dearborn, who was an original suspect in the bombing.

We shared something that few people could ever fully comprehend and none would ever desire to experience. It was a beautiful service in a quaint little church with traditional wooden pews and stained-glass windows. Candles were lit throughout the sanctuary as a symbol of life and the Holy Spirit in the midst of the darkness we felt. A Scottish bagpiper played *Amazing Grace*. It was a song that had always held particular meaning to me, being authored in memory of slaves in response to injustices they had suffered. A student at a Scottish College, I had grown accustomed to the sound of bagpipe music, and it awakened something in my spirit, probably linked deeply to my Scottish heritage. But now, it had even deeper significance with Scotland as the place of Ken's death.

Just being there at that service and meeting the others and seeing their tears began to chip away at the hard exterior that I was carrying. My heart began to come unglued, but the only thing I knew to do was to keep pressing forward. *If I could just return to life as usual, then maybe everything would be okay.* I didn't want to grieve. I believed that grieving somehow made Ken's death a reality. I was glad we had not gotten Ken's body back or had a funeral yet, because the lack of those things allowed me to keep Ken alive. The other Lockerbie family members shared a common love for their family members, but they had given in to the grief. I refused to do that.

Preparing To Grieve
Even though we had not received word of when Ken's funeral would be, Mom encouraged the family to attend a grief-counseling workshop that a local church was offering. Although resistant, my father agreed to attend, because he understood the importance for our family. Mom was particularly concerned

about me, because I hadn't cried and didn't want to talk about it. I was reluctant, but went out of a desire to support the other members of my family in their grieving process, still oblivious to my own need to grieve. The counselor taught us about the stages of grief that are common in the loss of a loved one. Rather than a counseling session, it was more of an informational workshop on what to expect in the coming months and years as things continued to unfold. The five stages of grief are:

- Denial: "This can't be happening to me." No crying, not accepting or even acknowledging the loss.
- Anger: "Why me?" Feelings of wanting to fight back or get even, at death, anger at the deceased, blaming them for leaving.
- Bargaining: "I promise I will be a better person if..." Bargaining often takes place before the loss. Attempting to make deals with God to stop or change the loss. Begging, wishing, praying for the loved one to come back.
- Depression: "I don't care." Overwhelming feelings of hopelessness, frustration, bitter- ness, self-pity, mourning loss of person as well as the hopes, dreams and plans for the future. Feeling lack of control, numbness, and perhaps suicidal.
- Acceptance: "I am ready to accept this." There is a difference between resignation and accep- tance. You have to accept the loss, not just try to bear it quietly. Realization that the person

is gone and that it is not their fault. Finding the good that can come out of the pain of loss, finding comfort and healing. (Elisabeth Kubler-Ross, "On Death and Dying," 1969, Touchstone Publishing)

Having an understanding of these stages helped tremendously in the coming months, when I started to melt down and thought that I might be losing my mind altogether. What that workshop did not prepare us for was that in a terrorist tragedy such as this, the grieving process could continue for many years.

Chapter 3 — My Family

"He and all his family were devout and God-fearing; he gave generously to those in need and prayed to God regularly." — Acts 10:2 NIV

From my very earliest memories, my family was characterized by a devout faith in Christ, uncompromising commitment to regular church attendance, a strong Midwestern work ethic, an independent spirit, and unwavering belief that we could do anything we set our minds to. Ken's death, however, rocked the very foundation of our faith and everything we had been brought up to believe.

My mother's heritage was German and Irish, while my father was Scottish, Irish, and Native American. The name Gibson is Scottish, and my ancestors came from Southern Scotland in the Dumfries and Galloway region, where Lockerbie is located and where Pan Am flight 103 found its final resting place.

We came from simple means, but we were always challenged to ascribe to greatness. My father, Larry Gibson was born in 1944 in Detroit, the youngest of Frances and Harlan Gibson's two boys. Grandpa Harlan was an alcoholic, which led him and Grandma Frances to divorce young. My grandmother single-handedly raised my father while she worked as a waitress at local fish-and-chips restaurant. Unable to support both children on her own, she sent my father's older brother, Gordon, to West Virginia to live with his Aunt Beatrice, Grandpa Harlan's sister. Times were tough, and Dad spent the better part of his childhood years growing up on the Penfold farm with my great-grandparents while Grandma worked multiple jobs to make ends meet. After high school, he went on to serve in the U.S. Marine Corps as a military policeman. He was stationed in Okinawa, Japan, during the Vietnam War and amazingly never served in the war itself. I often think that if he had, we kids would probably not be here today.

My parents were both 21 years old when they married in 1967, and their first child, my brother Ken, was born February 16, 1968. Dad was working nights as a machinist at a tool-and-die company called Kelsey Hayes in Detroit. Not long after they were married, my father came to know the Lord through a friend and co-worker. Shortly after that, he led my mother, Ruth, to the Lord and they began to attend a local church. From the very beginning, my father had an intense passion for learning about the Bible and theology. He went on to attend a local Bible college, and later went on to get his bachelor's degree in religion from Azusa Pacific University. But his desire for learning didn't stop there. He continued to take college classes and studied everything from business to computers, always returning to his first love of theology.

My mother grew up in a working-class home in Detroit. She was the only girl, with two older brothers, David and Jimmy. Her father was a "jack of all trades" and the sole bread-winner for the family. My Grandma Florence suffered from manic depression and schizophrenia for most of her life, from the time Mom was a child and into her adult years. At times, Grandma Florence was more functional than others, but the bulk of responsibility for up-keep of the home fell to my mother. Mom met my father through mutual friends while he was home on leave from the Marines. They wrote letters to one another until he finished his tour of duty. When possible, Mom worked full-time during our childhood. She even went on to get her associate's degree in accounting, which qualified her to work in higher-paying clerical and accounts receivable positions.

I was the first and only girl born to the Gibson family, on Good Friday, March 27, 1970. I always found a unique significance in the fact that the day I was born was the day Jesus died. Little did I know at that time the prophetic significance God had in that principle that with death comes life – and the impact it would have on my spiritual journey.

Ken was two years old when I was born. My mother had bonded so closely with Ken that when I came along, she worried about his resenting me. So she gave Ken most of the attention during those early years. As an infant, I was content to play quietly in my crib for hours. Not knowing any better, Mom assumed I didn't really need her and left me to myself. Consequently, I never really bonded and attached with my mother. As a child, I came to believe that love was conditional and that I was not allowed to have needs. I made a vow that if I was able to be strong and not be any trouble, maybe someday my parents would love me. The result was that I took on the role of being the strong caretaker of the family. Never able to be vulnerable, gentle or needy, the little girl in me never flourished. This continued to be my posture until well into my adult years.

There were four years separating my brother, Eric and I, and two years between Eric and Jason. In many respects, Eric's personality was a lot like Ken's. They were both borderline geniuses who never really applied themselves in school. Because of the similarities, Eric lived in Ken's shadow, always being compared to or mistakenly called by Ken's name. Because of these similarities, Ken was always really hard on Eric, not wanting him to make the same mistakes he had made. Jason was the youngest of the clan, and very much his own person. He was only 12 years old when Ken died, and because of the age difference between them, they were not very close during Ken's teenage years and after he left home.

A Family Of Modest Means

Despite having his bachelor's degree in religion, Dad continued to work in his trade as a precision-tool grinder who made parts for the automotive industry and other industries. Mom had to work a full-time job as well, for the family to be able to survive financially. Dad continued to go to school at nights to try to better himself. As a result, things got more and more tight financially as he took out loans to pay for the education.

We moved frequently during my early years for job purposes, which made it increasingly difficult to develop roots or security in life. It was really hard for me to make friends when I knew we would likely be moving again soon. I tended to involve myself in activities at school, but not in developing close relationships. After a while, being the new kid became second nature. As long as I didn't try to get too close, it wouldn't be that difficult when we left again.

The summer between junior high and high school, my Grandma Frances invited me to come and stay with her in northern Michigan. It is one of the fondest memories of my childhood, because being with my grandma always made me feel safe and secure. Though they lived on a fixed income, my grandparents always seemed incredibly resourceful, and there was never the fighting over financial issues that plagued my immediate family. I felt peaceful in the great outdoors of northern Michigan. At night, I would fall asleep to the sound of crickets outside my window. It reminded me of the few short years that we had lived not far from Grandma's house in

Black River, Michigan, where Dad pastored a small Free Methodist Church. That summer was filled with adventures. I was a lot like Grandma. She loved to stay active and was a bit of a tom boy growing up as well. I felt understood when I was with her, which was rarely the case with my own mother. We spent that summer fishing for suckers down at the old Red Bridge, perch fishing on their small boat on the Penfold pond and huckleberry picking in the woods. Grandma made the best fried fish and huckleberry pancakes. We would laugh, and Grandma would tell stories about her childhood growing up and everyday life. Grandpa Jack was more of a quiet soul, but he loved to come along as well.

That summer was, by far, the best summer of my life, and was crucial in my life journey. I had just finished my eighth grade year, and like most adolescents, I was a bit of a lost soul. But the year before that had been especially difficult. Our family had been living in Turlock, California, a small town about an hour's drive from Sacramento, where Dad was pastoring a Church of God congregation, which had a declining membership and suffered from church politics and financial troubles. Dad and Mom both had part-time jobs in addition to the pastorate, in order to pay the bills. Our family struggled more financially during our time there than ever before. One Christmas, things were so tight financially, we would not have had any presents had it not been for the Goodfellows, a charity that gives Christmas gifts to needy families. They provided a delectable box of goodies for our Christmas dinner, and clothes and toys for each of us kids. I felt no shame that Christmas, just complete gratitude for God's provision for us. I knew that one day, I would have the opportunity to turn around and repay that debt of gratitude by helping others in need.

During my eighth grade year, things at the church became increasingly tense, and there was a falling out between my father and the board of trustees. In the midst of that, my parent's marriage became increasingly strained. Mom and Dad were fighting more than ever. The straw that broke the camel's back came when my father was let go from the church. We were all extremely wounded, and our view of Christians and the church was greatly shaken. Dad got an extension for the family to stay at the church parsonage where we were living, until he could find another job. He had few options other than to stay with friends as he looked for a job as a grinder in Southern California, where most of such positions in California were located. For the first time ever in our childhood, discussions about divorce came up frequently. I was really scared about our future.

So when Grandma invited me to come for the summer and offered to pay for my plane ticket, I was ecstatic. I didn't know that when I left that summer to go to visit Grandma, I never would return to my house in California again.

That summer, my parents decided that their best option for saving their marriage was to return home to Michigan, where they could make a fresh start. They found a small house to rent in Romulus, a suburb of Detroit. Home to the automobile industry, this area provided the most prospects for my father to find work in precision tool and die. Tensions were still high between Mom and Dad, but they had committed to try to make their marriage work. My father hoped that a complete new start might breathe life into our family and our situation.

To afford the cost of the move, Mom and Dad sold most of our furniture and belongings before leaving California. I slept on a small blow-up mattress that slowly leaked until it was virtually flat. My bedroom had wood floors, which provided little cushion when the mattress lost its air. The few belongings of mine that made it to Michigan in the move remained in boxes on the floor. In the living room, we had a simple 1970s olive-green couch, a small television set, a lamp, and a table that we got from a yard sale.

Ken and I were responsible for taking care of our younger brothers much of the time, as Mom and Dad both worked full-time. We joined Lincoln Park Church of God in Lincoln Park, Michigan, and Ken and I got involved in the youth group. For the first time in my life, I felt some semblance of community with like-minded people my own age. I also got involved in many different activities as a freshman in high school. I played on the volleyball and softball teams and did well enough academically to become a part of the National Honor Society. I found contentment, purpose and meaning in performing academically, athletically, and in church and religious practice. I was becoming more confident and had more opportunities to develop my leadership skills. Although I still had very few close friends at school,

I began to make a name for myself in how I achieved. I was already thinking about college, and I knew my only hope was to do well enough academically to get scholarships to cover my tuition.

My Identity

At the depth of my personality, I have always been a strong woman with a bent toward leadership and performance. Like most people, part of the way I am wired has been a result of nature and some nurture. I primarily have a dominant temperament with a small part of me that is on the more passive side. I have the typical Type A personality. I have been very successful in achieving in my life, and much of my identity has been tied up in that. From my earliest memories, I knew I was not at all like my mother, who was more passive and submissive by nature. Feeling like I was not the kind of daughter Mom wanted, I focused my efforts on pleasing my Dad — an intellectual by nature, who most highly valued intelligence and performance in life and school.

A natural thinker, I enjoyed studies and learning. Debate was a normal part of life in the Gibson residence. So from a very early age, I became quite good at it. Standing up for people and against injustice has always been a core component of who I am. I was never one to get bullied at school, but often the one to come to the aid of others. On one occasion when I was in the fifth grade, I came to the aid of one of my classmates at school. We were in the girl's restroom and an older and much bigger girl, who was repeating fifth grade for the second time, decided to pick on my friend. She had my friend by the back of the neck and was threatening to stick her head in the toilet and flush it. Even though I was much smaller than the bully, I was overcome with a sense of courage to intervene. What she was doing was not right, and I wasn't going to just stand there and let it happen. Rather than intervening with violence, I chose the more logical route of persuasion. Somehow, I was able to convince the bully of her misguided ways. After some resistance, she relented and let my friend go. From that day forth, the girl who had been the class bully became my friend. She was misunderstood by most others, but I was able to see beyond the facade to her humanity. This gift would be instrumental many more times in my future, and would go on to influence the very direction of my life profession.

Our Faith Is Tested

I grew up in a family where we went to church three times a week, whether we needed it or not. We were in church Sunday mornings, Sunday nights and Wednesday evenings for the youth program. Unlike some children, I loved church. When Ken and I were 5 and 3 years old, we used to play church together. Standing on the stairwell looking down into our basement, Ken would play the preacher and I would be the music leader. I would belt out the song *Surely Goodness and Mercy* from the top of my lungs and Ken would proclaim "Hey all you people, Jesus loves all of you." Each day our imaginary church service would include the customary worship time, sermon and altar call. When I was 5 years old, I prayed to ask Jesus into my heart, and as much as a young child could understand, I took that decision very seriously and wanted to live my life for Him.

My earliest years were spent attending the Holiness Churches. Dad's faith was most influenced by John Wesley's theology, so we attended churches most aligned with this view. But we were not loyal to any particular denomination. Growing up, we were members of the Free Methodist Church, Wesleyan Church, Nazarene, and the Church of God out of Anderson, Indiana. The Holiness Churches were Bible-believing fellowships that focused on a salvation message, entire sanctification, righteous living, prayer and evangelism. Although we did not practice the fullness of the gifts of the Spirit, such as speaking in tongues and prophecy, we were a strong church in the area of prayer, anointing with oil and the laying on of hands.

Because of the emphasis on overcoming sin through living holy lives, our church upbringing had a strong legalistic bent. We were taught conditional security theology, which meant we believed you could lose your salvation. As a young person, I felt like any little slip-up could cause me to lose my salvation, so I tried my best to live the best life I could. From my earliest memories, I loved Jesus and believed He loved me. A very lonely child, I often felt that Jesus was the only one who really knew and loved me. In my darkest hours, as I would sometimes cry myself to sleep at night, I always felt His presence there with me and comforting me. But I grew up believing that Jesus' love for me was conditional. As long as I did what I was supposed to, He would stay. But if I did not, He would leave. I don't ever remember hearing teaching on God's grace until I became an adult. So, I lived my life like many Christians do. Bound to legalism, I lived my life to serve the Lord, praying that I could do enough to someday earn the fullness of His favor and love.

Growing up in the church, I saw the world through rose-colored stained glass windows. For the most part, I believed that bad things weren't supposed to happen to Christians. Our family struggled and my childhood wasn't the happiest, but we made do. Besides the occasional unexpected death of loved ones in our church family after months of concerted prayer, we never really had our faith tested in any significant way. I grew up believing that most of the really bad things that happened in people's lives were the result of bad decisions or their own sin. Merciful was not a characteristic that described my heart. I was committed to living my life with radical obedience and felt everyone else should do the same. I firmly believed that I could do anything I set my mind to, and that was the way in which I approached every aspect of my life.

Growing up a preacher's kid comes with added pressures that aren't customary of normal life. You are held to a higher standard than most children in the church. Always under constant scrutiny, most children of pastors either toe the line well or break under the pressure and rebel. My parents lived by the biblical principle that if you raise your children in the way they should go as a child, when they are adults they will not part from it. I followed the letter of the law during my childhood years, never rebelling even slightly. I was always seen as the good child, and at times my brothers resented it. What my brother's didn't realize was that the good child doesn't always draw as much attention as the ones who are getting into trouble, so sometimes I envied them.

When my family returned to Michigan from California, we had all been shaken a bit in our faith. We were in need of a fresh perspective. I grew by leaps and bounds at Lincoln Park Church of God. We had an outstanding youth leader named Don Peslis, whom we all deeply loved. The Bible came alive and we learned what it was like to live a life of service. Ken and I both were very active in the youth group, and our closest friends were there. I dated three different guys who were part of our youth group, and my best friend became Joann Fater. We both were athletic, playing softball and volleyball at school, and we had strong leadership skills. Quickly we rose to leadership roles in our youth group and became fast friends as we challenged one another in our spiritual walks. I had never really had many close friends in my life, so our friendship truly met a heart's longing in me.

Dad loved theology and prided himself on intellectual dialogue. In fact, he thrived on it. He enjoyed a good debate, and apologetics or intellectual dialogue suited him well. Always a bit dogmatic and opinionated, Dad had a tendency to like to challenge people in their faith or the way things should be done. Unfortunately, not everyone appreciated his approach, and at times, he rubbed people the wrong way. While we attended the Lincoln Park Church of God, Dad had some disagreements with the church leadership. During my senior year of high school, we left that church on less than good terms. I was grieved to be leaving the source of community I had developed in our youth group. For the first time in my life, I had close friends and now had to leave them. For a short while, our family went to another church. Not long after that, Dad stopped attending church altogether. Mom took us kids back to Lincoln Park Church of God, where we continued attending until I graduated from high school.

Living in a staunch Christian home, especially since my father was pastor, it was easy to rest my faith on my parents' faith. When I left for college, I had some decisions to make. My father had left the church, and for the first time he was exhibiting behaviors that I had not grown up with, including drinking. Dad was angry with the church, and in some ways with God.

I enrolled at Alma College, a Presbyterian College with a foundation of faith. But it was a pretty liberal campus where regular church attendance was not customary. My only regular spiritual involvement while attending college there was through the Fellowship of Christian Athletes. I rose up to be a leader in that group, but I was walking a fine line in my faith. I tried my best to stay the course in living the Christian life, but mostly out of fear of the Lord rather than out of passionate pursuit of His holiness. My first term went pretty well. I was a pre-law/political science major, and planned to graduate in three years. Taking a full course load while also playing volleyball didn't leave a whole lot of time for fun or partying. I began to date a guy who was two years ahead of me in school. He was on the swim team and loved to plan romantic, creative dates. Although he grew up a Christian, his faith was very impersonal. Distracted by the cares of life, my walk with the Lord became less of a priority.

When the Lockerbie bombing happened, my family's faith was already on shaky ground. We were Christians who believed in our hearts that God was sovereign, but struggled with why He would allow a tragedy like that to happen, especially to Ken. Many of our friends from our Lincoln Park Church community stepped in to offer comfort and support. In times of tragedy, Christians seem best able to set aside differences of opinion or hurts to help other members of the body of Christ in need. Through others' efforts to bring us meals or offer kind words of comfort and encouragement, we felt the power of the body of Christ in action, and it blessed us.

But there was internal wrestling with God going on. Like the story of Jacob wrestling with the angel in Genesis 32, there was an internal struggle going on in our hearts. Where was God in the midst of our tragedy? The enemy of our souls was hard at work trying to create doubt in our hearts where there had been faith. In some ways, we felt the depth of God's peace and grace, yet in other ways He felt distant and far off. Dad particularly struggled with guilt about the harsh words he said to Ken in their last phone conversation. I could see him vacillate back and forth between feeling shame and condemnation, to attempting to try to brush it off with pride. Asking God the tough question of "why" never seemed appropriate in our spiritual upbringing. So, my family tried to move in resolve to the circumstances at hand, never questioning God. But, I was uncomfortable with that approach. I needed answers, and for the first time I was angry enough with God to ask for them. Ordinarily compliant by nature, I was not going to be content with business as usual. My relationship with God and my very spiritual existence itself was on the line. From that point forward, my faith would never look the same.

Chapter 4 — The Aftermath

"What joy for those whose strength comes from the Lord, who have set their minds on a pilgrimage to Jerusalem. When they walk through the Valley of Weeping, it will become a place of refreshing springs. The autumn rains will clothe it with blessings. They will continue to grow stronger, and each of them will appear before God in Jerusalem." —
Psalm 84:5-7 NLT

After the New Year, and about two weeks after the bombing, I returned to school to start the second term of my freshman year. My college was a three-hour drive from my home, and my parents were worried about me being so far away from the family during a difficult time like that. Still in denial, I was anxious and determined to try to return to life as usual. I told my roommate and closer friends what had happened, but I really didn't want to discuss it much further.

Always looking for world events to use as object lessons, both my political science professor and my speech professor brought the Pan Am bombing up in class. My speech class was on nonverbal communication, and the teacher used the bombing as an example of a form of nonverbal communication. "What were the terrorists trying to communicate through the bombing?" he asked.

Good question, I thought. *What on earth could possibly compel someone to blow up a plane full of innocent people?* It was the first time I had allowed myself to ask that question. My political science class was on international relations. Unaware of my connection with the Lockerbie bombing, Professor Monshipouri stood up and made justification for the bombing based on the belief that it was in retaliation for the bombing of an Iranian passenger airline. Monshipouri was an Iranian national and a devout Muslim. As I sat and listened, tears started to well up within me. *Keep it together,* I told myself. It was the first real emotion I had felt since we found out the news. *This isn't some abstract discussion. This is my brother we are talking about. How dare he?* I wanted to raise my hand and say something, but I couldn't. I was frozen with fear. I knew that if I opened my mouth, I would lose it. I could feel my temperature rising and my face turning beet red. I did not know for sure what would come out of my mouth, but I knew it wouldn't be good. So I quickly gathered my books and belongings and walked out of the class. I ran straight back to my room. My room-mate had class as well, so fortunately I had the room to myself. I sat down in the chair next to the window as the tears streamed down my face. Anger, outrage and contempt rose up within my spirit. I knew very little about Islamic terrorism and the views of it in the Koran. But the thought that any right-minded person could stand in front of a room and condone such an egregious act sent my temper through the roof.

I wanted desperately to go and confront my professor, but I was afraid. My emotions were starting to come unglued, and I had no idea how I would respond. Feeling somewhat unbalanced and afraid to broach the subject with him directly, I decided to write him a letter. It was rather simple, and I tried to downplay the emotion I felt. I merely conveyed that my brother Ken had been killed on the Lockerbie bombing and that I thought it was inappropriate to justify the actions of the terrorist. In my pre-law classes, Professor MJJ Smith had already begun to condition us that when presenting an argument, our feelings are irrelevant. We don't "feel" but "believe." So, to the best of my ability, I presented my argument. Writing the letter helped me get the outrage I was feeling off my chest.

Professor Monshipouri received my letter via interoffice mail the day after I sent it and called my dorm room immediately to request an in-person meeting. I was scared to meet with him to discuss it because I wasn't by any means feeling rational or calm. He had a very strong, non-emotional, Middle Eastern disposition that made him a bit intimidating to me. But I agreed to meet with him the following day. In the meeting he was nice and apologized for his words because he did not know my brother had been killed on the plane. He said he wished I had said something in class. I assured him that though I wanted to, but it would not have come out well at all. It was a brief meeting, but one that was important for me to have. Just talking about it, although I was still somewhat emotionally removed from it, was good for me.

In the meeting with Professor Monshipouri, I got to see a bit more of the human side of him. In class, he was always very professional and serious. It was often difficult to grasp his humanity in that context. But in a one-on-one meeting, he seemed more down to earth and real. I appreciated hearing a bit more of his perspective and worldview on the issue of terrorism. At the time, they were speculating the bombing might have been in retaliation for the U.S.'s accidental shooting down of an Iranian passenger airplane. As an Iranian and a Muslim, Professor Monshipouri had a different perspective. From his perspective an "eye for an eye" would be appropriate. Of course, it is easy to condone such an act or even terrorism in general, until you are sitting face-to-face with a victim. Then the reality of it makes it all a bit more complicated. I could see that in his posture of interacting with me. Although we did not discuss it in any detail, at the time I was aware that as a Muslim, there was a good chance that he might support jihad or holy war as an integral part of the Islamic faith. I wasn't ready to embrace that possibility if it was true, so I ended our meeting short of going down that road with him.

Two days after starting back to school, I was sitting in my speech class when the dean of students pulled me out of class. He said he had just spoken to my family. "Your brother's body is arriving tomorrow," he said. "You need to go home for the funeral."

I was almost speechless. "Thanks," I said. Then I returned to my room and gathered my belongings. I had my own car on campus, so I packed up and headed home. Still on autopilot, I drove as fast as I could. I had no idea what to expect or why I was in such a hurry. But deep within my heart, any last grain of hope that remained was beginning to fade away. *Soon I will know for sure if Ken was on the plane.*

Denial — No Longer An Option

Days before Ken's body was returned home, Dad spoke with the general of Ken's company in Germany. He informed Dad that anyone we chose would be available to escort Ken's body back and be there for the funeral. We didn't know any one specific person, so Dad asked if Ken had a close friend. The general mentioned that Jim McCoy, Ken's room-mate, was his closest friend. So Dad asked for Jim to escort the body back. Our thought was that spending time with Jim would give us an opportunity to fill in many of the blanks that we were unaware of while Ken was away.

On January 4th, Ken's body arrived at Detroit Metropolitan Airport and was delivered to the funeral home. Grandma and Grandpa drove down from up north to be there when we went to the funeral home. We had no idea what the condition of Ken's body would be. The funeral home still did not know if his body was viewable, but they wanted to know if the family wanted to see it if it was not. Dad, Grandma, and Eric gave an emphatic "yes." Mom and I were unsure. So the mortician went to view Ken's body to determine the condition. "There has been extensive cosmetic work, but he is viewable," he said. They laid Ken's body in the viewing room and invited us in for our private viewing.

I was dumbstruck and lingered at the back of the room. I didn't want to go up there to see him. But Mom insisted. So as a group, our family walked to the front. When I laid my gaze upon his body lying there in that ornate casket, I let out a wail. "No, no, that is not my brother, that is not my brother. That is some kind of mannequin!" I cried.

It was the first sign of emotion my family had seen from me since the news of the bombing. I began to melt down and my knees buckled beneath me. Mom tried to hug and comfort me. But she was glad, too, because she had been worried that I had not exhibited any emotion before this point. Finally, the door of denial that kept my heart secure swung wide open, and the well of emotions sprung forth and flowed like a river.

Filling In The Details

After the private viewing Ken's body, we left the funeral home and went out to a Denny's restaurant for dinner with Jim McCoy. It was our first opportunity to meet him, and we were all very eager to learn more about Ken's life during the previous year and a half that we had been apart. It was our first of such meetings over the course of the next week, where we were able to process, laugh, and cry together. I immediately felt close to Jim, like he was family. He had a kind disposition and seemed quiet by nature. He was very gracious with us as we flooded him with questions about every aspect of Ken's life.

The first meeting was low-key, as we were all still reeling from the reality of finally seeing Ken's body. But over the course of the following days, we asked many questions, desperate to grasp every detail of Ken's life that we could hold onto. What was Ken's life like in Germany? Did he enjoy his job? And most importantly, was he still walking with the Lord?

Jim talked about how excited Ken had been to come home, and that the night before he left, Ken kept him up all night talking. We could hear in Jim's voice that Ken had found purpose in life and a new sense of pride that he was anxious to share. He had just been invited to attend the West Point Prep School, which was preparatory school for select enlisted Army members who were interested in becoming officers. Ken was also pursuing an opportunity to be a part of the Ranger Program, which is an Army Special Forces Program.

Jim also gave some insight into Ken's social life. We knew Ken had been dating a German girl, but what we hadn't realized was that Jim and Ken were dating twin sisters. Jim was engaged to and later married the other sister. Ken's girlfriend was planning to come home with him, but at the last minute backed out.

As we reminisced, Jim even shared some funny stories. Always a difficult one to get up in the morning, Ken had a bit of an addiction to the snooze bar on the alarm. Jim said Ken had found the perfect alternative to the traditional alarm clock. He had a baseball alarm clock that turned off by throwing it against the wall. Ken had worn out three of those clocks in less than a year. We all just laughed and laughed as we were reminded of Ken's humanity in the middle of the chaos of our tragedy.

One of the biggest questions we had about Ken was where he was in his spiritual walk. He always had a thriving relationship with the Lord while we grew up, but in recent years while being away, he didn't share as much. We were still living under the doctrine of conditional security, so there was always a measure of concern as to whether he was right with the Lord when he died. My parents were looking for some outward manifestation of faith in Ken's life they could hold onto. Jim was able to provide that. I was already beginning to question the legalism that we had grown up under. I knew that Ken had accepted Christ and really believed it, so I believed whole-heartedly that Ken was in heaven. I could see my parents' complete countenance change as Jim assured them that Ken still talked about his faith. It gave Mom and Dad tremendous peace to know that although they lost their son, he was in a much better place.

A Final Resting Place

Ken's body was laid out for one day on January 5th, and the funeral was held on January 6th. Having grieved some the day before, I was more composed the day of the viewing and the funeral. We stayed at the funeral home most of the day of the viewing. As countless friends and family came, we took them up to the casket. Even complete strangers who had heard about the tragedy would come to share their condolences. The most unexpected guest was a general from the Pentagon who came to offer his condolences. "The reason I am here is that the U.S. considers this an act of war," he told us.

I felt like we were introducing the attendees to Ken as we escorted them up to the casket, always preparing them in advance for the obvious cosmetic repair that had been done. To me, Ken's body was a shell, but I understood the importance of seeing it. I even took pictures of him in the casket that I look at from time-to-time or share with others and to keep my memories fresh.

Ken had once told me that if he ever died, he wanted Don Peslis, our former youth leader, to conduct his funeral. In hindsight, his request was quite strange, because as a teenager, death is rarely seen as something immediate. I have often wondered if there had been some level of "knowing" within his spirit when he shared that request. Don happily agreed to come in from Anderson, Indiana, to offi-ciate Ken's funeral.

Every one of our family and friends were so blessed to see Ken have a full military funeral. One of the members of the color guard who was assigned to the funeral found out upon arrival that he had known my brother Ken from Boot Camp at Camp Benning, Georgia. "I knew Ken and really liked him," he told us. "It is an incredible honor and privilege to be a part of his funeral."

Don did an excellent job officiating the ceremony and giving the sermon. Because he knew Ken intimately, he was able to interject many heartfelt stories and anecdotes about Ken. He referred to Ken and his two closest friends in our youth group as the "Three Amigos." Always a bit of a "Jesus Freak" among his peers, Ken tended to hang out with some of the "burn-out" types and rockers. He led more than one of his non-believing friends to the Lord by taking them to a Christian rock concert. Don's fondest memory of Ken was seeing him pulling into the church parking lot with the windows down and the Christian rock band *Stryper* playing full blast on the stereo.

As expected, the media showed up at the funeral and the reporters wanted to come inside the funeral home. My parents felt that was inappropriate. So they agreed to let them stay in the parking lot across from the entryway. But we kids didn't realize they were there. We stood by the double doors getting ready to leave. When the doors swung open, about ten to fifteen reporters and their news crews were standing with their cameras perched to take pictures. Usually the quiet one of the family, Jason yelled, "Why are they here? They have no right to be here." It reminded me of the paparazzi who follow movie stars around, trying to get newsworthy pictures of them in very personal moments. We huddled together and made our way to the funeral home car that would take us to the cemetery.

As the funeral procession pulled out onto the main street, I noticed there were several police motorcycles escorting the procession. They were driving back and forth along the side of the procession as we proceeded to the cemetery in Flat Rock, Michigan, for the burial. It reminded me of the scenes I had seen on television of the presidential motorcade as it moved throughout a city.

As we neared the cemetery, another funeral procession was approaching the intersection on a cross street; our police car and police motorcycle escorts raced ahead to block the intersection so that our procession could take precedence. *Oh, Ken, you would be so proud.* I felt that somehow he knew and was looking down from heaven.

At the cemetery there was the color-guard ceremony, which included the playing of *Taps*, presentation of the colors, the gun salute and presentation of the flags to my parents and grandparents. The color guard ceremony was the most moving part of the entire funeral. As *Taps* was played, I broke down. *This is really it. Oh, God why couldn't I have at least said good-bye?* I was lost in my thoughts as the ceremony came to an end. Because it was winter, the cemetery had to hold off on burying the casket until spring when the ground thawed. Without seeing the casket put into the ground, we left.

I only returned to the cemetery on one future occasion. Our family visited Ken's grave together on

May 31, 1989, the first Memorial Day after his death. I knew in my heart that his spirit was no longer there, so I never returned again.

After the funeral, we drove to Aunt Amy and Uncle Steve's house for the funeral dinner. It was a time of eating, drinking, and remembering. The mood was more joyous than somber. Though we would never again have the opportunity to see Ken in this lifetime, we found comfort in the fact that he was in heaven. Still, I was left with this lingering sense of non-closure because the person responsible had still not been found, and I had never had the chance to say good-bye to my brother. Don Peslis gave me a tape by Bebe and Cece Winans, which included the song, *Bridge over Troubled Waters*. It brought me tremendous comfort in the months to come when I was hurting and my faith was faltering.

Chapter 5 — The Grieving Process Begins

"God blesses those who mourn, for they will be comforted." — Matthew 5:4 NLT

I remained at home for the two days following the funeral, doing my best to help support my family with any loose ends that were outstanding. But deep within me there was a burning compulsion to return to school. After all, what good would it do me just to sit at home? Planning to graduate from college in three years, I knew that every day I stayed at home put me further behind. Despite my family's wishes, I insisted on returning to college. "At least at home we have each other," Mom urged. But I was insistent. In my mind, the best thing I could do was to just push through the grief I was feeling and to throw myself into school. It seemed like the right thing to do because I was oblivious to what lay ahead.

Returning to school this time was much more difficult. I was no longer in denial and was knee-deep in
grief. The stages and emotions of grief seemed to hit
me in a less than linear fashion. One moment I would
be feeling sadness and the next anger. My thoughts
and feelings were all jumbled up somewhere between
my heart and mind. As a private person, I felt it best
to keep most of what I was feeling to myself. *No
one would really understand,* I kept telling myself.
I didn't understand myself, so how could I communicate to others in a rational way? Yet, I also longed
to have a friend I could just talk about Ken with and
remember the happy stuff. So much of the grieving
process involves reminiscing about your loved one,
but I had no idea how to broach the subject. College
is supposed to be a light-hearted time of parties and
fun, interspersed with the occasional class or home-
work assignment. Plus, none of my classmates knew
Ken. I felt like most people in my sphere of influence
resented the tragedy that I had gone through, and the
seriousness of my posture. Most college students
have never dealt with anything remotely as tragic, so
they had no idea how to relate. Instead, they would
have preferred for me to just snap out of it.

This included my boyfriend, Todd. From the first
news of the tragedy, he had begun to withdraw. Upon
my return to school, the person that I should have
been able to turn to for support and encouragement
the most broke up with me. Initially, he just avoided
me and then when I finally confronted him, he ended
our relationship completely. I was devastated. Rather

than reaching out to family or for professional help, I became increasingly withdrawn.

For most of my life, I had felt alone, but now I was not only alone, but daily losing more and more control. In times past, during my loneliest moments I had felt God's presence. But now, I was angry with God and didn't trust Him. I was bombarded with many different emotions, but hopelessness was the prevailing one. I missed Ken so much that I began to contemplate my own death and how much better things would be if I could just be with him in heaven.

I was failing miserably at my effort to focus myself on my schoolwork. At times, I was in so much anguish that I would skip class and simply sit in my room and weep. I was in a pit of despair and I could not seem to climb out. Mom became increasingly concerned about my inability or unwillingness to talk about what was going on with me. When we would talk on the phone, I would put on airs that I was doing fine and spend the whole time talking about everyone else in the family. But unlike other times in my life, where I successfully pulled the wool over her eyes, this time I couldn't. She knew that I was desperately in need of help. So she called the school's counseling department and told them the whole story and asked them to force me to come in and talk to someone. Of course they couldn't force me, but they did call me and urge me to come in. At that point, I knew I was spiraling downward, so I agreed to go and meet with the counselor.

The counselor was a woman in her early thirties. I was deeply stressed about the prospect of even having to go see a counselor. All I wanted was someone who could help me keep it together. I shared as much as I could articulate with her, without sharing the depths of the despair I was in. My biggest fear was that if I was completely honest with her, she would want me to leave school and go home. Performing in school felt like all I had left, so I couldn't risk it. I went to a total of two counseling sessions with her. In the last session, I shared with her that the most significant area of anguish I was feeling was not being able to say good-bye to Ken. She had no answer for me. Instead she encouraged me to find outlets for the stress I was feeling. "When I was in college, I used to find long hot showers were a great way to relax and de-stress," she offered.

Hot showers? This woman has absolutely no idea the torment I am in! That was the last time I met with her. I realized if I was going to make it through that term, nothing short of a miracle was going to do.

Pressing In To My Coursework

Part of my original decision to attend Alma College was my pre-law advisor, Dr. MJJ Smith and his "three-year plan." Most college students do their undergraduate education in the standard four years, with the occasional student who decides to do their undergraduate education in five years. But getting an undergraduate degree in three years is almost unheard of. Why would anyone want to try to do it that quickly, when they could stay at college and enjoy all the fun activities that go on there?

Only an overachiever would ever think of trying to do their undergraduate degree in three years while still working part-time. When I met Dr. Smith he proposed this opportunity. Each student takes a four-credit class with him during the summer, a minimum course load of 19 hours during the fall and winter terms, and a four-credit class for each six-week spring term. The benefit to me as a student was that I would get out of college a year early, have one less year of student loans, go onto law school sooner, and be out making the world a better place in no time flat. I also loved the challenge of doing my under-graduate degree in three years, something few people had undertaken. That challenge was more important to me than the party lifestyle of fun activities that are the typical part of the college years. It would be tough, but as long as I stuck to the plan and was focused, I could achieve it.

When I returned to college that second term after Ken's death, I had a tremendous difficulty staying focused. A more prudent person would have assessed the situation and made a decision to forego the three year plan. But I was determined and driven to follow through with what I had set out to do. My advisor and parents tried to encourage me to lighten my course load and give myself some time. I bull-head-edly refused their counsel. I was going to stay the course and succeed with what I had committed to do, or die trying. Unfortunately, I almost did kill myself in the process. Alma College was a tough school and

I was carrying 18 credit hours with classes in British literature, history, political science, physical science, speech and religion. Unable to stay focused on my assignments and studies, I fell increasingly behind. I would bounce back and forth between sulking in the sea of despair and pressing forward on my assignments with blind determination. I had difficulty sleeping. I was a basket case emotionally, and stressed beyond all comprehension.

That term, my grades suffered and I received a 2.39 grade-point average, which was the lowest I had ever had in my life. In high school, I was a leader in the National Honor Society. This GPA was completely unacceptable. I was absolutely devastated. A good GPA was imperative for admission to a good law school. So from that point forward, I spent the remainder of my time at college desperately trying to increase my GPA.

The Battle In My Heart

There was a drastic change in my behavior between my first semester and my second semester. During my first term, I was playing volleyball on Alma College's team, was dating a great guy, and enjoyed being apart of school activities like football games. During my second semester, I was a recluse by day and started going out to parties with my friend Robyn on weekends. Robyn and I had lived across the hall from one another during our first semester, and didn't particularly like each other. She was a dance major and her course load was pretty easy while mine was intense. She spent more time hanging out with boys and partying than on actual academics. But during my second semester, when I was a bit unstable, she was one of the few classmates who was understanding and supportive. I really appreciated how she would allow me to just be where I was at, even if it wasn't particularly attractive or rational.

I found myself increasingly in need of a way to let off steam and release the stress I was experiencing. Working out helped some, but ultimately Robyn convinced me that I just needed to go out and have some fun. So on the weekends, I spent the days playing catch-up on my schoolwork and the evenings out partying. Fraternity parties and the bars seemed the best way to deal with my blues. Being a good Christian girl, I did my best to keep myself from getting too out of hand, but there were a couple times where I woke up the following morning with little memory of what transpired the night before. That really put the fear of God in me, and I knew that God definitely must have been protecting me, even in the midst of my stupidity. The sense of shame I felt for my behavior would be quickly replaced by the feeling of abandonment I felt from God. *Where was He in the midst of my sorrow? Did He even really care?* I was angry, alone and beginning to question God's love for me.

God Meets Me Where I Am

At the heart of the anguish and despair I felt over my brother's death was the fact that I had never had the chance to say good-bye to him. When people die of old age or even after being sick, family and friends have the opportunity to speak with them before they pass on. They can share all the things that are on their hearts that they never had the chance to say, and most importantly they can say good-bye. There is something very important in the healing process for a loved one in being able to say good-bye. Too often we live our lives by holding back on sharing things with people we love, until it is too late. Maybe it is our pride, fear, or self-absorption. But we count on those last minutes before our loved ones pass away to share all the things that have been lingering in our heart. Sometimes we even wait to share Christ and the gift of salvation with them until they are on the doorsteps of death.

In the case of a sudden death, you are robbed of the opportunity to share those last dying words. It was only after losing someone so dear to me as my brother that I began to change my whole perspective. Tragedy shakes you and causes you to see things from a much different perspective. Life truly is short, and you never know when someone you care about may be snatched from you. So I realized that from that day forward, I had to live in such a way that I never put off telling my love ones something that was on my heart or in my mind. I needed to share it then, because I might never again have the opportunity. I never had the chance to tell Ken how much I admired and respected the man he was turning out to be, and how I admired his heartfelt faith and desire to share it with others. Living with that level of intentionality is different and even counter-cultural. But I had learned the hard way that it was the only way to live.

A Vision From Heaven

The sticking point in my grieving process seemed to be my inability to say good-bye to my brother Ken. I would lament continuously to the Lord: *If only I had the chance to say good-bye, then maybe I could move on.*

One afternoon during spring term, I was sitting in my friend's dorm room watching the Oliver North hearings unfold. It was a warm day and the sun was shining brightly through the glass windows of her dorm room. As I sat there, with my eyes affixed on the television, I experienced what seemed at the time to be the remembrance of a dream. But rather than a distant thought or memory of the night before, it was quite vivid and appeared as though a movie was being played back to me in my mind's eye. To that point in my life, I had never experienced anything like it. The closest thing I had to such a vision was the picture I saw of a plane exploding the night before the bombing. But this vision was different, because I was a part of it. It was as if I was aware of my surroundings but simultaneously experiencing the vision that I was seeing. I later learned that it is called an "open vision."

In this vision, I was sitting on a park bench in this very surreal setting. All the trees and grass were a deep green color and the flowers were in bloom. There was a small stream flowing behind the park bench and a light fog and mist in the air, but the temperature was perfectly comfortable, as on a typical spring day. The birds were singing softly in the distance and I felt a peace like I never had before.

Then a car pulled up in the parking lot. It was a red Chevy Camaro sports car and there were two passengers inside. As I looked at the car curiously, the door to the passenger side opened and out came my brother Ken. My heart leaped expectantly as though I had been expecting him. As he approached the park bench, he had a comforting smile and looked the way I had last seen him. He came and sat beside me. I had never felt so happy.

I asked him about the guy in the car and he told me that he was dead, too, and had been killed in a car accident. I was anxious to try to find out more about the Lockerbie bombing. I asked him what happened and who was responsible. But he simply responded that he could not tell me that.

"Ken, there are so many things I have wanted to tell you. So many things that have happened in my life," I said. I felt like a little girl again, talking to her older brother.

"Lisa, I know about those things. And there are going to be times when the family is going to be together and I will be there with you," he said.

"Don't be sad," he said. "I am in a much better place."

I knew in my heart that he was. I could see the peace all about him, and I was comforted just by being in his presence. After talking a bit longer, Ken informed me that he had to go. As he prepared to leave, we stood up and he gave me a hug. I felt the warmth and security of his embrace. It was as real to me as any hug had ever been. Somehow I knew in that moment, that from that day forward, things were going to be okay. Before he drove away, I shared my parting wishes: "I love you, Ken, and will miss you."

"I love you too, sis," he said. It was a simple good-bye, but no less heartfelt.

After the vision was over, I sat there quietly with a new sense of peace I had not felt in quite some time. It was as if the dark cloud that I was under had been lifted. For the first time in the almost six months since Ken's death, I was basking in the goodness of God. I felt bathed in God's glory and a sense of joy began to penetrate my wounded heart. I soaked up the feeling of peace and tranquility that was all about me. I told my friend who was there in the room with me what I had just experienced. I did not completely know what to make of the experience or how to articulate it. She just looked at me in disbelief, unable to make sense of what I had just experienced.

I felt my experience was deeply personal. It was a special gift from God to me. I knew few would understand it, since I didn't even fully understand it. I knew I should be careful who to share it with in the future. The one thing I knew for sure was that God had heard my heart cry. *Maybe God hadn't abandoned me after all.*

Chapter 6 — Season Of Questioning

"The righteous perish, and no one ponders it in his heart; devout men are taken away, and no one understands that the righteous are taken away to be spared from evil. Those who walk uprightly enter into peace; they find rest as they lie in death." — Isaiah 57:1,2 NIV

My college years after the Lockerbie bombing began a season of questioning that continued for many years. It was both a spiritual and intellectual quest for understanding. But unlike the typical life questions that I was trying to navigate as a college student, my questions this time around were different and much deeper.

When you lose a loved one in a tragedy, it is common to be left with questions. But when you lose someone in a crime or intentional terrorist act, you can't help but have every idealistic and optimistic view of the world shattered. Unlike an accidental plane crash, the terrorist who blew up Pan Am 103 was trying to communicate a message of hate. At the root of my search was an attempt to make sense of it all.

Idealism Shattered

I had always considered myself an idealist, with the cup always being half-full. Even in tough times, I looked for the good in situations and the rainbow at the end of the road. But losing my brother in the Lockerbie bombing rocked my worldview. I am a thinker by nature and so in order for me to effectively navigate situations, I need to understand them. My father always valued intellectual dialogue, debate and questioning as an effective pathway to truth. In fact, this methodology is at the heart of the Socratic method of teaching that I became quite versed in when I later went on to law school. I have always been one to ask a lot of questions because I have a curious streak. But in my heart, I am also always trying to improve things and make them better. I am a natural change agent. In order to improve things, you need to have a thorough understanding of the way something works. Only then can you effectively make recommendations for change. It is like that old adage, "If it ain't broke, don't fix it."

I found myself struck with questions such as why did the bombing happen? Why did God allow it? Why specifically did it happen to my family? But there were also more fundamental questions about the nature of God, such as why would a good God allow such a tragedy? Why does God allow suffering? Did our family do something to bring this upon ourselves, or was God punishing us?

A fatalist would look at Ken's death through the lens of chance, luck or karma. Muslims have an extreme view of fatalism that describes their perspective. The most common phrase to hear a Muslim say, is "Insh Allah," which means "If God wills it." They look at the world through this lens, and it shapes every aspect of how they live their lives. From their perspective, if God desires it to happen, it will happen. If he does not will it, it will not happen. So, if something bad happens, it must have been God's will.

As a follower of Christ, I knew without a doubt that God was sovereign. He was all-knowing and ever-present. So, there was no evil act that happened without His knowledge. I understood from the story of Job that Satan wasn't even allowed to bring suffering upon Job, a righteous man, without God's permission. So, at least in part, that Scripture would support the proposition that even acts of evil or bad things that are brought upon mankind had to go through God's approval first. If that is the case, then God not only knew the Lockerbie bombing was going to happen, but He allowed it to happen. That was a lot to wrestle with.

As I read the Bible growing up, I saw the wrathful side of God. He was often angry, and on more than one occasion He called forces to destroy people He was unhappy with or who were disobedient. But the God of the New Testament was supposed to be different. I was brought up to believe that He was a loving God. And because of the blood that was shed for my sins by Christ, I could approach the throne of God's grace with confidence. Hebrews 4:16 NIV says, "Let us then approach the throne of grace with confidence, so that we may receive mercy and find grace to help us in our time of need." Though I didn't fully understand the idea of grace, I did know that grace meant God's unmerited favor. He was, after all, Father God. What father wouldn't allow his hurting and confused child to come and sit before him and allow her to ask him those many lingering questions that were on her heart? My view of God's goodness was wavering. I needed to have my view of God restored. I knew that God would want that, too. I believed in that humble posture, there was no question too difficult or big for God to answer. My quest for answers began.

Wrestling With God

The search for my spiritual questions began with the Bible. After all, what better source to really understand the fullness of the nature of God than His written word to His bride, the Church? Much of my early biblical learning had focused on the dos and don'ts of Scripture and the stories Christians typically first learn in Sunday school. But we often skipped over the books of the Bible like Lamentations, which is an entire book about the Israelites expressing their anguish and despair to God. Lamentations 3:37 NIV says, "Can anything happen without the Lord's permission? Is not the Most High who helps one and harms another?" Verse 31 says, "For the Lord does not abandon anyone forever. Though He brings grief, He also shows compassion according to His unfailing love. For He does not enjoy hurting people or causing them sorrow." Yet, this book of the Bible seems to be about the children of Israel's lament based on judgment God was bringing upon them. What about those situations where a person has experienced a tragedy through no fault of his or her own?

The Psalms also seem to be full of as many verses expressing anger or despair toward God as they do joy. Through most of the Psalms, you see David running for his life, hiding out in caves, and experiencing betrayal. In Psalm 22:1, 2, David says, "My God, my God! Why have you forsaken me? Why are you so far from saving me, from the words of my groaning? O my God, I cry by day, but you do not answer, and by night, but I find no rest."

One of my favorite stories in the Bible is the story of Jacob wrestling with God in Genesis 32:22. So often our tendency as Christians is to wrestle with the cares and concerns of life with our backs to God, rather than engaging Him directly. In this story, Jacob engaged God in a full battle and wrestled with Him all through the night. When it became clear He would not win, God dislocated Jacob's hip. He was left with a limp, but in the end Jacob received his blessing. This story perfectly illustrates that there is a cost to engaging with God. But because God is a relational God, He desires us to engage with Him as we struggle with the challenges of life.

We know that God is by nature a just God. The idea of justice in a biblical context relates to someone getting what he or she deserves, whether as punishment or what is rightly done to someone. So where was God's justice in my brother's death? We had not done anything to bring it upon ourselves, so why had it happened? I found myself acting as a spiritual defense attorney as I pled my case in heaven's courtroom. Our family had been directly attacked by a group of people we did not know, but nonetheless they saw us as enemies. I found myself resonating with David in Psalm 25:19 NLT: "See how many enemies I have, and how viciously they hate me!" He pled his case to God in Psalm 27:7,8 NLT: "Hear me as I pray, O Lord. Be merciful and answer me!" And God heard David's plea. "My heart has heard you say, 'Come and talk with me.' And my heart responds, 'Lord, I am coming.'" I needed to hear those same words that David heard from God: "Come and talk with me."

Time and again, we see God responding favorably to His children when they call out to Him in their time of distress. As I searched the Scriptures for answers to my spiritual questions, I didn't necessarily come up with the answers I was looking for. Instead, what I found was a bigger view of the complexity of the world we live in. I also gained more revelation about the character and nature of God in relation to the difficult times and tragedy we experience in our lives. I was starting to realize that tragedy and suffering were part of the package of being in God's family. But in the midst of it, God promised to be our ever-present help in time of need.

Understanding Terrorism

Very early on in the investigation, it became clear that the bombing was a result of Islamic terrorism. Officials were still investigating which country or terrorist group was responsible, but it definitely fit the profile of Islamic terrorism. More than one terrorist group took responsibility for the bombing, as if it were bragging rights. Initially, it was believed that Iran was responsible for the Lockerbie bombing and that it was in retaliation for the United States government's accidental shooting down of an Iranian passenger airplane. Later, the investigation turned to the country of Libya.

At the time, very few Americans knew much about Islamic terrorism. Far removed from our radar screen, terrorism was not yet a household word. So one of the most consuming questions I wrestled with in my quest for understanding was what would compel a group of people to blow up a plane full of innocent people? It wasn't necessarily a new concept, but it was new to us as Americans. Countless other countries had been dealing with it for years. These were the days before Internet, so finding readily accessible information on terrorism was difficult. I found myself digging through microfilm newspaper articles from different nations around the world, trying to learn anything I could about terrorism.

Through the 1970s and into the 80, hijacking of airplanes became an increasingly common act of terrorism. Then in the 1980s, plane bombings seemed to be more popular. There was the bombing of the Berlin disco, the 1986 French airliner bombing over Niger and countless others. Also during the 1980s, hostages were kidnapped in Iran and held for more than a year. Several of the hostages were Americans, including a relative of one of my neighbors in Azusa, California. I was nine years old at the time and remember thinking about that young man often and praying for him, despite never knowing him personally. Though I was still very young when it happened and did not really understand, it was the first event that caused me to think about terrorism.

I had seen kidnappings on television shows, and the kidnappers always asked for a ransom. The Iranian kidnappers didn't ask for a ransom. Unaware that I would one day revisit this issue, I was simply left with the question: Why did they do it?

But because terrorism had not yet touched American soil or impacted a large group of Americans, we paid little attention. Be it ignorance or ethnocentric self-absorption, we just felt immune from it.

My political science and pre-law course work centered on international relations and world politics. We studied events in the geopolitical world and were more aware of what was happening than the average person. But I was hungering for something deeper as it related to the Middle East and North Africa. It was no longer theory to me — it was deeply personal. As my senior year approached, I began thinking about the prospect of doing my senior thesis on international terrorism. I had Professor Monshipouri for a couple more classes after my first class with him freshman year. As an Iranian and a Muslim, he had a much different worldview than most Americans. It was quite surprising that he was even serving at Alma College, a white Anglo Saxon Presbyterian college located in a town known as Scotland, USA, in the middle of Michigan farm country. Diversity, especially as it related to international students, was almost non-existent at the time. At times, his domineering Middle Eastern tendencies would come through, which made him a bit intimidating to me. But I knew that if I were to tackle the project of doing my senior thesis on international terrorism, that he would serve as the advisor on the project and provide oversight.

I was a bit fearful about approaching him about the project. After all, I wasn't by any means objective about the topic. He knew that. Did it even make sense for me to take it on? How could I separate my personal feelings in my quest for understanding? But I likened it to someone who lost a loved one to cancer doing a research project on cancer. Certainly that person could separate their anger and outrage at the disease for killing a loved one.

But this was different. This had been an intentional act of terrorism by a person or group of people directed at innocent people. Was it really possible for me to distance myself from my personal loss to understand the roots and motivations of terrorism? I wasn't completely sure, but I wanted to try. If for no other reason, perhaps I could learn enough to somehow prevent similar acts of terrorism from happening in the future.

I was surprised to find Professor Monshipouri very supportive of my desire to do my project on terrorism. Unlike me, he wasn't at all concerned about my objectivity and thought my personal connection would make it all the more meaningful. He said he had seen me in class settings and trusted that I was fair and teachable. In the end, he was confident that I would come out with a solid heartfelt project and a broader worldview.

Professor Monshipouri and I set out clear terms for the project. In order to make it more objective, I should focus my study not only on Islamic terrorism, but terrorism in general. Then I could contrast Islamic terrorism with other terrorist acts. What made them different? How were they similar? What were the roots behind them? These were the kinds of questions I was trying to answer.

At the time, the most well known terrorist acts outside of the Middle East involved the Irish Republican Army (IRA) in Ireland. For years, this organization had been involved in many egregious acts of violence in Northern Ireland. The roots of terrorism in Ireland were religious — the Catholics were fighting against Protestants. But there were also political components at work. The roots of terrorism in Ireland were for governmental control and influence. Many of the perpetrators of the terrorist acts in Ireland were unhappy with the social circumstances that they found themselves in, and were recruited to participate in the IRA as an outlet for that discontent.

It is true that throughout history, many terrorist acts have been perpetrated in the name of religion or because of ethnic or political differences. The Crusades led by the Catholic Church in the 10th century resulted in many atrocities against Arabs and Jews over a period of 200 years. In Rwanda in the mid 1990s, the Hutu majority group committed mass slaughters of the minority Tutsi group in one of the worst genocides ever recorded in history. During the mid to late 1990s, Joseph Koney's "Lord's Resistance Army" raped and pillaged countless towns in Uganda, forcing children into military service. In Darfur, Sudan, since 2003 there have been countless people killed by Islamic militants, many connected with the Northern Sudan Government, in heinous acts of terror. And of course one cannot forget the mass extermination of countless Jews at the hands of Adolf Hitler during World War II.

Terrorism is the intentional attack upon innocent people that is designed to cause fear and communicate a message. What differentiates a legitimate freedom fighter from a terrorist is sometimes a fine line to discern. At the root of terrorism is hate. In rules of war, military troops are to do everything in their power to avoid the loss of innocent non-combatant's lives. Islamic fundamentalists see themselves at war with everything that is associated with Western culture. They see Western nations as propagating secular influences that are counter to everything Muslims believe in. Muslims view the freedom in democratic societies as a catalyst to sin. Movies coming out of places like Hollywood promote hedonism and secular humanism, which are counter to everything Muslims believe in.

Understanding Islam

To understand the struggle between Islam and the West, one must understand a little bit about Islam. The word Islam comes from the word "salam," which means peace in Arabic. It also means submission to the will of God for peace in this life and in the afterlife. The Holy Books of Islam include the Qur'an, Hadith, Psalms, Torah and the gospel known as the Injil in Islam. Islam is considered an Abrahamic religion like Judaism and Christianity. But Islam comes through the lineage of Ishmael, Abraham's first son born to Sarah's maid-servant, Hagar. As such, Islam retains many parts of the Old and New Testament as holy books of Islam.

The Qur'an is the Islamic holy book that is considered to be a miracle from God revealed to Muhammed directly from Allah.[i] Since the Qur'an came into existence in a chiefly oral culture, it was not collected into book form during Muhammed's lifetime.[ii] Instead, "it was preserved by his companions who recited, memorized, practiced, and transcribed it."[iii] It was later compiled in its first official written version around 634 AD. The earlier chapters of the Qur'an, called suras, communicate a more tolerant attitude toward Christians and Jews. Jerusalem was the original holy city of Islam, which is also the case for Christians and Jews. Early Muslims prayed facing

Jerusalem. Later suras reflect a shift from identifying with the traditions of Christians and Jews to establishing Islam as a distinct religion itself, with Mecca as its center of worship. Today Muslims pray in the direction of Mecca.

Muslims also rely on the Hadith, which is the record of what Muhammed and his early companions are known to have done and said. These writings serve as a guide for Muslims on how to live their lives. The collected traditions include things like moral teaching, religious duties, and legal problems.

Islam is first of all a legal system and second a religion. The rules and principles taken from the Qur'an and Hadith were codified into a fundamental legal system of Islam called Shari'a. Several Islamic countries base their governing constitutional law on Shari'a. Like most legal systems, there are different schools of thought on how Shari'a is to be interpreted.[iv]

The basic tenets of the faith of Islam are known as the five pillars of Islam. These include the Shahada, the Muslim creed or confession of faith that says "There is no god but God (and) Muhammed is the Prophet of God."[v] The second is Salat, or the five daily prayers, to be performed at sunrise, at noon, in the mid-afternoon, in the evening, and at night.[vi] Saum, or ritual fasting, is the third pillar that happens during a 40-day period known as Ramadan, during which a Muslim allows no food or liquid to pass down his throat during the daylight hours. From nightfall until dawn, Muslims are permitted to eat and drink. Not participating in the fast is seen as a defiance of the communal moral code.[vii] The fourth pillar is Zakat, or giving of charity to the poor. It is done as a form of purification of oneself from the guilt that comes from accumulating property.[viii] The fifth pillar is the Haj, or pilgrimage to Mecca. Every devout Muslim tries to fulfill the obligation at least once during his or her lifetime. During Haj, pilgrims flock to Mecca from all over the world.[ix]

Sometimes regarded as another duty of Muslims, or even the sixth pillar, is jihad.[x] The basic meaning of the word is "struggle for the faith." The stipulations for jihad are found in Sura 2:190-193. The English interpretation says, "On behalf of God, fight whoever fights you, but do not be the aggressor; indeed, God does not like aggressors. Kill them when they advance on you and force them out of the places from which they forced you... Fight them until there is no persecution and religion belongs to God, and if they abandon their ways there is to be no hostility — except against evildoers."[xi]

Two kinds of people are cited as being objects of such activity — those who do not believe in God at all and pay no regard for what he has prohibited (Sura 9:29), and Christians, who "ascribe partners to God"(Sura 2:135).[xii] Islamic fundamentalists justify militant Islam on the basis that they believe the West is encroaching on everything that Islam holds dear. Therefore, fighting back in jihad is done merely in self-defense. The roots of Islamic terrorism are found in the Muslim concept known as jihad, which some also call holy war.

Just like there are many different Christian denominations and degrees to which people understand and follow the faith, the same is true of Islam. There are Sunni, Shia, Sufi, Wahabi and other branches of Islam. And within those branches are those who consider themselves religious and others who are secular Muslims. Within the religious Muslims are individuals and groups more fundamentalist in nature. Some Muslims follow the law of Islam to the letter and others just use it as a guide for their lives.

Today approximately 85 percent of all Muslims are Sunnis, while 15 percent are Shi'a.[xiii] The initial and fundamental split between the two was over the question of succession to Muhammed. Because Muhammed made no provision for his successor, a crisis in Islam ensued.[xiv] Shi'a believe that only a relative of Muhammed could be the legitimate successors, who would have the title of Imam, while the Sunnis believe that the consensus of the community should determine the selection of the leader they call the Caliph.[xv]

The Islamic Caliphate was the leadership structure for the Muslim world for almost 1300 years. [xvi] By the eighth century, about 100 years after Muhammed's death, the authority of the caliphs extended over parts of three continents, from what is now Pakistan across the Middle East and North Africa to what is now Spain and Portugal.[xvii] Most of the jihadists repeatedly claim that the ultimate goal of their violent struggle is to restore the Islamic caliphate.[xviii] This Caliph is often referred to as the Mahdi, a Muslim Messiah-type figure.[xix] The idea of reinstating the caliphate is the way many of the Muslims struggle with the dissatisfaction with politics in the Muslim world today.

At its roots, Islamic terrorism is perpetrated for a political or ideological goal and is designed to communicate a message of fear. Religion is sometimes the primary motivation, but it is also used in combination with other factors. Terrorists intentionally attack innocent people. They target well-populated areas, such as planes, trains, restaurants or office buildings.

Suicide bombings have become one of the most common forms of terrorism. Islamists believe that dying as a suicide bomber for the cause of Islam guarantees the highest honor from Allah. From a very early age, young men are brought up believe that if they die in jihad, they will be guaranteed a place in paradise and receive 70 virgins and will be able take several of their closest family and friends with them to paradise. Dying in jihad is the only guarantee for a Muslim to make it to paradise.

The two people groups that Islamists have set their targets upon are Jews and Christians. Judaism, Christianity and Islam all contain similarities at least in part of their holy scriptures. Initially, Muhammed was exposed to Christian teachings through rogue Christian groups and believed that he was called to take Christianity to Islam. The Qur'an was developed from writings over the course of many years, but there is a principle in Islamic faith that says later writings replace earlier writings where the two are contradictory. Although earlier writings of the

Qur'an referred to Christians and Jews as people of the book and encouraged good relations with them, later Qur'anic scriptures spoke of Christians and Jews less favorably. Sura 9:29-30 says, "Fight those who believe not in Allah nor the Last Day, nor hold that forbidden which hath been forbidden by Allah and His Messenger, nor acknowledge the religion of Truth, (even if they are) People of the Book, until they pay the Jizya with willing submission, and feel themselves subdued. The Jews call Uzair a son of Allah, and the Christians call Christ the son of Allah. That is a saying from their mouth; (in this) they but imitate what the unbelievers of old used to say. Allah's curse be on them: how they are deluded from the Truth!" As the years passed, the teachings of Islam became increasingly less tolerant and more critical of Christians and Jews both in the Qur'an, the Hadith and by individual Imams or Sheikhs, the religious leaders and teachers within Islam.

Simple Answer

After finishing my senior thesis, I knew a lot about the history and ideology behind Islamic terrorism. But in my spirit I was still not content. It just left me with more questions. I did not even want to try to rationalize or justify it anymore. I asked the Lord for His guidance. As I sat there silently, He spoke to my heart these words: "Lisa, the answer is quite simple. We live in a fallen world and the only answer is Jesus Christ." It was a simple answer to what seemed like an insurmountable question. Yet somehow it made sense. Evil and hate are real, and Christ is the answer.

If I was somehow going to prevent terrorism, I needed to be a part of seeing Muslims come to Christ. At least that much was clear. It was an interesting prospect, but one I wasn't quite ready for. Other than my Iranian professor, I did not know any Muslims and frankly, that was the way I wanted to keep it. For the time being, I was content being indifferent toward them.

Chapter 7 —
Disappointment, Loss And Survival

"I have told you these things, so that in me you may have peace. In this world you will have trouble. But take heart! I have overcome the world." — John 16:33 NIV

As my senior year of college came to a close, I found myself in a much different place than I ever would have imagined. I had worked as hard as I could to rebound my GPA after the poor showing during my freshman year. But all my efforts left me with was just over a 3.0 GPA, which was unacceptable for a good law school and barely acceptable for a mediocre one. To make matters worse, I scored a 21 on the Law School Admission Test (LSAT), and that score was average at best. Even after taking a LSAT improvement course, I scored in exactly the same percentile the second time around. Try as I might, I just couldn't get a hang of the symbolical logic questions on the exam. They drew upon much of the same analytical process that was required for math. Although I leaned toward being more of a logical thinker by nature, math had always been a subject I struggled with.

After months of applying to every accredited law school I could think of, the results were grim. Law schools by nature are extremely selective, and I just wasn't measuring up. In the end, I was only admitted to one law school, Thomas Cooley Law School in Lansing, Michigan. It was a little-known private law school that was founded by former Michigan Chief Justice Thomas Brennan. His vision in starting Cooley was to offer law school education to individuals who ordinarily, might not have the opportunity. It was easy to get in, but very difficult to stay in. Because of Cooley's open-admission policy, there was a year-long waiting list to start. So there I was, having busted my butt to get through college in three years, only to be waitlisted for a year for the only law school that would accept me. I was beyond discouraged. To make matters worse, because Cooley was private, it was more expensive. Any hope of receiving any scholarship money was shattered, so I knew my only hope was to work to offset the student loans I would have to get. My only option was to move back in with my parents for that year and find two jobs so I could save as much money as possible.

Returning Home

After Ken's death, Mom and Dad received proceeds from Ken's life insurance policy that allowed them to buy a home in a nice neighborhood in Canton, Michigan. Although the house was nice and they allowed me to stay there rent-free while I was waiting to start law school, I felt like I was returning home in defeat. At times during college, Dad would make critical comments about my need to do better and work harder if I was going to get into a good law school. Although Dad's comments were made with good intention, they only further reinforced my drive for performance and approval. But of course, I was working as hard as I could. I knew that. Ken's death and the accompanying circumstances had derailed the plans I had for my future and I resented it. All the while believing that my plans were to use my education to serve God, I felt anger and resentment toward God as well.

After Ken's death, my family seemed to wander further away from God. As the cares of life pressed in, each of my parents felt less and less connected to the body of Christ. Only my brothers, Eric and Jason, continued to go to church.

Being an officer in our local Fellowship of Christian Athletes Chapter had been the extent of my spiritual involvement in the years after Ken's death. When I returned home from college, I had no immediate plans to become involved in a local church. Although I still considered myself a Christian, I felt disconnected from God at a heart level. Much of my faith growing up in the church was connected to the faith of my parents. So when my parents left the church, I didn't see any real reason to continue. In my heart, I felt that God had let me down. God didn't care enough to help me get into a good law school. So if I was going to be successful, it looked like I was going to have to do it myself. Maybe one day when I had done enough to serve God, He would love me. For the time being, I thought I needed to focus on working even harder than I ever had before.

Immediately upon returning home, I began to look through the newspaper for a job. Since I knew that I was only available to commit to an employer for a year, I looked for positions that called on my previous office and clerical skills, but also required a bit more of a challenge. I started out looking for secretarial jobs with law firms, but then stumbled upon a position with a local insurance agent. The office was two miles from my home, the subject matter seemed interesting and the staff was friendly. The pay wasn't great, but the hours were from 8 am to 4 pm, which would allow me to find another job working nights at a local restaurant.

It was a bit challenging, returning home and attempting to enter back into the family unit, but not because I didn't get along with my family or because it cramped my independence. After all, I was working all the time and didn't really have any close friends to socialize with. It was difficult because being at home was an ever-present reminder of my brother's death. Initially, the tragedy brought my family closer together. The tense relationship between Mom and Dad was put on hold for the betterment of the family. Ken's life insurance policy provided enough money for my parents to make a down payment on a home in a nice neighborhood. The hope was that maybe starting over again might turn things around for our family.

But as the days lingered on, the stress of the ongoing investigation and lawsuit caused tensions to rise and deep-seated wounds began to emerge. Mom and Dad grew further apart. Dad was struggling with guilt over the way he left things with Ken and the fact that he never had the opportunity to make it right. The last time Mom had spoken with Ken, she told him that she and Dad were going to try to make their marriage work. So for another five years she hung in there, keeping that promise to her lost son. They say that a parent should never have to bury a child. Statistically, parents who have had their child die are far more likely to divorce than parents who have not. Few could understand the grief that a parent feels, especially when their child is murdered.

Amid the stress of it all, Mom and Dad turned on one another. As a result, they began arguing more than ever, which made living at home like living in a war zone. They tried marriage counseling, but they weren't jointly committed to the process. Shortly after I left for law school, they legally separated but continued to live in the same house for financial reasons. My youngest brother Jason, a junior in high school at the time, was the only child left at home and had to weather the tumultuous storm alone. At one point, he even considered becoming an emancipated minor so he could move out of the house. During my second year of law school, they finalized their divorce. I was sad it ended that way. I knew divorce was not God's best for them. Yet, my hope was that they could both finally find peace.

Lawsuit Against Airline

The bombing investigation was ongoing, and it seemed like every day brought another key development or piece of information to light in the saga. The idea of closure seemed a very distant reality. Evidence came out that Pan American Airlines was negligent in its screening practices of passengers' luggage that was carried on the plane. So the Lockerbie families entered into a class-action lawsuit against Pan Am Airlines. As the details unfolded, it became clear that the luggage carrying the bomb traveled unaccompanied on the plane. The airlines had failed to apply the baggage reconciliation procedures. In addition, Pan Am had received a letter warning of the bombing and did nothing to engage in extra security procedures. Although bomb-screening technology was still more primitive at the time, Pan Am Airlines had recently purchased scanners that might have detected the plastic explosives that were in the bomb. Unfortunately, the new scanners were not being used on the day of the bombing.

The prospects seemed good for a favorable judgment for the Lockerbie families. But financial burdens of our new house began to press in when Dad lost his job. As a result, he felt he had no choice but to accept the settlement from Pan Am Airlines rather than wait out the lawsuit, which ended up taking several more years. Although finances can't solve all problems, they can help to minimize them. So that settlement helped to provide a bit of relief from the pressure on our family for a short season.

Law School

In May 1992, I began the process of moving to Lansing, Michigan to start law school at Cooley. Through the law school's housing department, I was matched with two roommates who were also starting their first term of law school. One roommate was from New Jersey and one from Grand Rapids. Kendra was just a year older than I, while Mary was about 10 years older. We found a three-bedroom apartment in East Lansing, Michigan that was the perfect place for the three of us.

We started night classes in June. Cooley had the largest student body of any Michigan law school and was located in downtown Lansing near the state capitol. Despite its large student body, the school itself was located in three buildings within a three-block radius.

On the first day of orientation, we were all filled with expectation and fear. Most of us had read the book *One L* by Scott Turow, which is a story of a student's turbulent first year at Harvard Law School. So we had a good idea of what the first year of law school was going to look like, and it wasn't good. I sat next to my two roommates in a room of more than 350 people. Within minutes of being introduced to my fellow classmates, the process of jockeying for position began. I had known that law school would be competitive, but I didn't necessarily understand what that would look like. Everyone recognized that

Cooley had an open admission policy, so the way to make yourself stand out among the others was to talk about the caliber of the college you went to or the other law schools you were admitted to. I knew that Alma College was a fine academic institution so I focused my talk on that school and tried to avoid the question about other law schools I had been admitted to.

As President Brennan gave his introduction to our class, he made a comment that resonated deep within me. "Look to your left and then look to your right. Because there is a good chance that the person you are sitting next to won't be here come graduation time." My heart sank. *Oh God, please let that not be me.* I couldn't bear the thought. I knew I had to succeed at law school because my very future depended upon it.

I started to develop an interest in law during my senior year in high school. In my government class, we studied many areas of the law and I had the opportunity to participate in a mock trial. I quickly rose to the front of the class as an effective advocate and prided myself on the ability to present myself in a formidable way during our debates. During our mock trial competition, I was the lead "counsel" tasked with arguing in opposition to a policy that required people with AIDS to wear arm bands to identify themselves in a manner similar to the stars that Jews wore in Nazi, Germany. I had never found anything that charged me with such a sense of meaning and purpose as that. It wasn't just the debate or argument, but it was the heart-felt conviction that there was such a thing as right and wrong and that justice should prevail. I felt empowered that deep within my being was a call to be a voice for the voiceless. Proverbs 31:8,9 NIV became my life verse. It says "Speak up for those who cannot speak for themselves, for the rights of all who are destitute. Speak up and judge fairly, defend the rights of the poor and needy."

Ken's death also served to further catalyze my desire to go to law school. During that time, we were still living the day-to-day evolution of the investigation. Not only was I learning the principles of jurisprudence that would prepare me to one day practice law, I was also learning foundational legal principles that were shaping my worldview of the Lockerbie investigation. I wanted to become a prosecuting attorney who would intervene on behalf of victims of crimes and see their perpetrators brought to justice. I could think of no higher call. In my heart, I saw a connection between my ability to right others' wrongs and righting the wrong against my brother and other bombing victims.

I entered law school with a very idealistic view of the legal system and everything it was about. What I found was an institution that was not designed to teach us about the idea of justice, but instead to help us to think critically about the law and to argue effectively. No longer were right and wrong so clear. Instead, she who won was she who made the best argument. That is why law school teaches you to lay down your own convictions and simply look at the facts, apply the law and make an argument for the outcome that best represents the needs of your client.

In that context, the attorney's feelings or convictions are irrelevant and an attorney can argue the case for any client or cause. In the midst of a culture of relativism and compromise, I was determined to hold fast to my altruistic visions for going to law school. I wanted to leave the world a better place than I found it.

My years in law school were even more consuming than the previous years of college had been. I was going to school full time year-round, while also working a part-time job. Over the course of my two and a half years, I worked for a health club, a lobbyist, the law school bookstore, a construction company, and finally for a law firm. The rest of my time was consumed with classes and studying. I was overworked and sleep-deprived. On average, I got about four to five hours a sleep a night, which is barely enough to survive on.

There was no time for God or the spiritual disciplines of the Christian life. Law school is all consuming, which causes people to be self-centered. That is likely why many marriages fail while one spouse is attending law school. My prayers were almost exclusively centered around me and my studies. More often than not, my prayers were simple pleas for God's help and strength to make it through each day. The verse "I can do all things through Christ who gives me strength" became my mantra. I knew that I could not rest on my own laurels if I was to make it through law school successfully. Although my faith was weak, I knew that the Bible only required a "mustard seed" size of faith. I clung to that.

My intimacy with God wavered. I see it much like a marriage — if you neglect your spouse and your time together, you will feel disconnected. I was neglecting my first love during that season, despite wanting nothing more than to succeed in law school so I could serve God with my degree. I still saw my identity in Christ as being about doing things for Him, rather than being with him. Law school continued to reinforce that pattern of thought. Achievement was the sole focus.

Most often the hyper-competitive environment brought out the worst in students desperate to achieve a competitive edge any way they could. We had one exam at the end of each term to prove ourselves. Since exams were graded on a scale, it was each woman for herself. Because of the nature of the workload and course work, sometimes working in groups was necessary. In that interdependent environment, we had to work with others to get through but still keep enough distance so that we could maintain a competitive edge.

In the end, it was unwise to trust anyone. This made authentic friendships and relationships very difficult. My roommate Kendra and I became good friends and a support system for one another. But deep down, my heart felt very alone.

Chapter 8 — Desert Experience

"O God, you are my God, earnestly I seek you; my soul thirsts for you, my body longs for you, in a dry and weary land where there is no water." — Psalm 63:1 NLT

Due to the all-consuming stress of law school, most of my classmates turned to partying as an outlet for their stress. Since I saw the danger of going down that path, I looked outside my law school community for a distraction. In my free time, I enjoyed working out at the gym. It seemed the most healthy way to blow off steam, and I was able to interact with people who had nothing to do with my law school. It was refreshing. I also found myself looking to relationships with men to fill the loneliness, boredom and spiritual void I felt in my heart. For so long, my heart needs had been neglected. It was a valid need, but the wrong approach.

Without any Christian guys to be found, I turned to dating men who were fun, lighthearted, and adventurous. As long as they were spiritual, I seemed to be comfortable dating them. I found myself losing more and more focus on Christ and being more influenced by New Age principles and practices. The power of positive thinking became my religion. Unfortunately, New Age spirituality doesn't have the same commitment to morals and character values that are part of the Christian walk. I found myself compromising my values in ways that were not honoring to God on more than one occasion in those dating relationships. That left me feeling empty and further distant from God. The final blow came when a guy that I had been dating for six months dropped a bomb on me. He informed me that despite what he had originally told me, he was not divorced, but still legally married and in fact had two children. This came in the midst of my most intense time in law school and my own parent's divorce. I was not only angry with this man for lying to me, but with myself for not seeing his true ways. Rather than running to God with my grief, I ran away from Him and further into myself.

Law School Graduation

I managed to complete law school in two and a half years, and graduated with honors in December 1994. I was incredibly proud of myself, but it seemed somewhat anti-climactic. I was already thinking about the bar exam I was scheduled to take in February 1995. I had no downtime between law school graduation and the beginning the two-month bar review class and intensive study schedule. I continued to clerk full-time for the law firm until two weeks before the bar exam. It was an unrealistic endeavor, but I thought I could do it. I would work from 8 am to 5 pm Monday through Friday and then study for the bar exam from 7 to 10 p.m. during the week and at least 10 hours a day on the weekends. The last two weeks before the exam, I studied for 12 hours a day. The rigor of the schedule took its toll.

Four days before the exam, I noticed a pain in my chest and back. At first I wondered if I had pulled a muscle because my book bag was too heavy. But then it became increasingly difficult take a deep breath. I felt shooting pains throughout my chest and when I tried to lie down on my back, it was unbearable. The day before I was scheduled to sit for the bar exam, I was diagnosed with walking pneumonia. I was prescribed antibiotics and anti-inflammatory medicine. After two months of studying, I had no intention of backing out of the exam. Despite being unable to sit up completely straight in my seat or take a deep breath, I took the exam. A month and a half later, I found out the news I feared the most. I had failed the exam by one point.

Somehow failing the bar exam by twenty points might have been a bit easier to deal with. But one point was so close. One point is like a penny — it is almost negligible. And unlike the CPA exam, when you fail the bar exam, you have to take the whole thing over, not just the section you failed. I was completely demoralized because I had never failed anything before. But failing the bar exam seemed like the ultimate failure. I was afraid to tell my Dad, and couldn't imagine having to take the exam again.

I knew Dad would be critical, but I had no idea the extent to which his words would wound me.

When I called to tell Dad the news, I was already in tears. I had felt this deep lump in my throat. I had to tell him then, or I would lose the courage. As I picked up the phone to dial Dad's number I was shaking.

"I gave 100 percent and I did my best, Dad. But I failed the exam by one point," I said.

"Well, your best isn't good enough," he said. "You have to do better"

My heart sank like a deflated balloon. *How could I do better than my best?*

"If you spent as much time studying for the exam as you did crying, maybe you would have passed."

There wasn't even an ounce of compassion in his voice. I was completely crushed and enraged at the same time. I responded with a four-letter expletive that I had never used with my father before, hung up the phone and then tore it off the wall. I sat there alone in my apartment and wept uncontrollably. I not only felt like a failure, I was a failure. My father's words confirmed it. I never would have expected such cruel words from anyone, especially my own father. For several days, I was completely depressed and withdrawn as I wallowed in a sea of despair.

I didn't know what else to do other than to try again. Not only was my future on the line, but my identity was, too. I had no intention of letting the enemy, nor my father's cruel words, take me out permanently. With all the determination I could muster, I yanked those arrows from my heart and pressed into overdrive, beginning to study for the next bar exam in July. What choice did I have? Until I passed the bar exam, I couldn't start working full-time as an attorney. If I didn't pass the bar exam, I would spend the rest of my life working as a law clerk, never allowed to represent a client or argue a case in court. It was one of the scariest prospects of my life. And I understood that the longer a person waits to take the bar exam after law school, the more difficult it is to retain the information you learned and pass the exam.

I didn't have the luxury of taking time off from work, because I had to pay my bills. As a result, studying for the second exam was much like the first. I worked full-time and studied in my free time and on the weekends for three months straight. Despite my best efforts, it was not enough. In late August, I learned that I had failed the bar exam again.

When I made the decision to go to law school, I never fathomed that I might fail the bar exam. To fail it not once, but twice, was inconceivable. How could I get through law school with honors and then not be able to pass the bar exam? All the dreams I had were teetering on the edge of destruction. For the first time in my life, I knew that the words, "You can do anything that you set your mind to," were a complete lie. I had worked and studied as hard as I could, but it simply wasn't enough. In that moment, I hit the lowest place I had been in my life. Every ounce of strength that I had once possessed was now gone. I couldn't even muster the will to try again. I was simply maxed out, and I found myself waving the white flag of defeat.

One night I sat alone in the quiet of my room and cried silently. I couldn't even produce deep tears of anguish anymore. "Dear God," I prayed silently to myself, "I can't do this anymore. I give up!"

I heard Him speak into my spirit. "Good, now I have you where I want you."

"God, all I have ever wanted was to serve You. I simply wanted to become a lawyer so I could make the world a better place, but I failed You."

"My daughter," I heard Him say, "I can't use you when you are like this. Because as long as you insist on being in control of your own life, I can't be in control."

Those gentle words of rebuke penetrated deep within my heart, and the tears of sorrow began to flow. Somehow in my quest to serve God, I had lost sight of God himself. I was trying to serve God, without involving Him in the process. It was the ultimate place of arrogance to think that God needed my help. Yet God showed me that I was trying so hard to earn His unconditional love that He had already freely given to me. I felt His spirit bathe me with the unconditional love of a father. It was unconditional love that I had never really experienced or had lavished upon me. Scriptures I had read in years past began to flow into my head. "The Lord is close to the brokenhearted and rescues those who are crushed in spirit."(Psalm 34:18 NLT) "Cease striving and know that I am God."(Psalm 46:10 NASB)

In that moment, I was moved to repent for my independent spirit and pride in trying to serve God without His help. I felt the peace that passes all understanding flow over me like a wave at high tide. I felt completely refreshed.

In the days that followed, I thought almost nothing about the bar exam or my future. I had been living in a dry and weary land without any water. I needed deep spiritual food from the Word of God and living water from Christ's spirit. For so long, I had been working and striving so hard, I simply had no idea how to just "be." I found tremendous comfort in Matthew 6:25: "Therefore, I tell you, do not worry about your life what you will eat or drink or about your body what you will wear. Isn't life more important than food and the body more important than clothes? Look at the birds of the air, they do not sow or reap or stow away in barns and yet your heavenly Father feeds them. Are you not much more valuable than they are?" Verse 34 says, "Therefore do not worry about tomorrow, for tomorrow will worry about itself." Though I didn't fully understand how to live a life like that, I wanted it. I found myself almost envying the birds of the air and their light-heartedness. My heart had been anything but light-hearted, but I hungered for that.

About this time, I had started to develop some health problems. I had a small rash above my left cheek that would become red and inflamed. I was also continuing to struggle with the painful pleurisy that was initially believed to be related to walking pneumonia. Pleurisy involves inflammation of the chest cavity surrounding the lungs, which causes shortness of breath and sharp shooting pains when breathing. My physician referred me to specialists for further testing. I was diagnosed with discoid lupus and further testing indicated that I was believed to have systemic lupus as well. Lupus is an auto-immune disease where the body essentially turns on itself — the good cells in the body attack other good cells. The result is inflammation among the joints and internal organs. Pleurisy is one of the many ways Lupus manifests itself. The long-term prognosis was unclear. To make matters worse, my insurance company refused to pay my medical bills, alleging that I had a pre-existing condition based on symptoms that had begun before my insurance policy went into effect. I found myself deeply troubled about my future.

As I was sitting alone one day, I began to yearn for a new perspective. So often my spiritual walk had been characterized by doing things for God, I simply had no idea on how to just be with God. I always knew God was a relational God, but the thought of God caring more about His children being with Him than doing things for Him was difficult to grasp.

"Come away with me," He whispered into my spirit. *Where? I need a complete overhaul of my perspective, but where can I find that place of solitude and peace?*

Into The Desert

Growing up with Native American blood, I had always been intrigued by the "vision quest" on which Native Americans went. It was a spiritual journey where they went into the desert for a time of solitude, prayer and fasting, where they could hear from God and gain His vision for their lives. It was a pilgrimage most often taken during a time of transition or deci-sion-making. Always a lover of the outdoors, I knew that going into the desert would truly nurture my soul and allow me to hear more fully from God on His vision for my life. So I got on the Internet one day and began to look for a program like that. I signed up for the one that took groups into the high desert of California and included a three-day solo time where the group members would spend time fasting and praying. Perfect, I thought, since I had rarely prac-ticed the discipline of fasting, I knew that being out in the middle of nowhere would insure that I followed through with the fast.

I was filled with anticipation when I arrived in California for my vision quest. I met up with the four other women who would also participate. We were five sojourners, each from different backgrounds, but each in search of some vision for our lives.

Although I had lived in California for six years while growing up, I had not spent any time in the California desert. It's a beautiful place with rolling terrain but little vegetation. Sagebrush rolls about the land as it does in old Western movies that I grew up watching. I could even smell the tranquility of that place and as the wind blew through my hair, I felt carefree and a deep sense of peace just being there.

On the day our solo time began, each lady ventured out to find her place of solitude. It was a water-only fast and we took only the bare essentials of sleeping bag, clothes and a tarp. We left even our watches behind. That way there would be nothing to distract us. I also took my Bible and journal, hoping for divine revelation for my life.

Because we were in the desert, the nights got very cold. I took lava rocks that were natural to that terrain and heated them in the fire and put them inside a pair of my socks. I slid them into the foot of my sleeping bag to keep warm at night. As I drifted off to sleep, I could hear coyotes howling in the background. I had never experienced anything like it. In the solitude of nature, things seemed to make so much more sense. It was all divinely created and connected.

At dawn I awoke to the sound of birds singing loudly. It was as if they were singing only for me. My heart was flooded with joy like it never had. I was reminded of the birds again from Matthew 6. *Oh God, how I love the birds and wish my life was like them.* "You can, just open your wings and fly," I heard the Holy Spirit say.

For the first time ever, my heart was filled with unspeakable joy. The little girl inside of me, who had so long been repressed, came alive. I danced and sang and explored the desert floor. Beautiful desert flowers were in bloom everywhere and the warm sun beat upon my face. Somehow in my imagination, the desert had never looked so beautiful. I found myself laughing for no apparent reason. A new-found light-heartedness came alive in me as I just fellowshipped with the Holy Spirit. I was experiencing a little slice of heaven that I did not want to end.

I had gone on the vision trip seeking direction for my future. Instead, I came away with a child-like spirit that I had never expected. The inner compulsion to strive and perform had been softened. I no longer felt like I had to work to earn God's favor, because for the first time I felt His favor. His goodness was all around me, and I could not get enough of it. I still had no idea about the direction for my future, but that was okay. I was at peace for that season and would trust God for the timing and details.

For six months I had a reprieve from the bar exam. I continued to clerk for the same law firm and focused my efforts on areas of spiritual development. But I knew that if I was going to use my law degree to practice law, I would have to take the bar exam again. After much thought and prayer, I registered to take the Georgia bar exam. Many of my friends from law school had moved to the South after law school, and I thought maybe Georgia might provide a new perspective and start for my life.

So I registered to take the February bar exam in Atlanta. I studied for the exam as I had before, but I had a much different perspective. My mind was clear and I seemed to be able to focus like I never had before. There was no longer any fear. The night before I was to take the exam, I slept the most restful night of sleep. God's grace was upon me and despite the rigor of sitting for the two-day exam, I felt no anxiety. I was completely at peace.

Six weeks later I learned that I passed the bar exam with flying colors. I was ecstatic, but I knew I could not take the credit. It was God in me who had allowed me to pass the exam, and it was He who deserved all the honor and glory.

Like the children of Israel, I found myself wandering in a spiritual desert for many years. My heart's desire was to serve God, but in my pride I wanted to do it my way, probably so I could take the credit. But that experience taught me that in our brokenness and humility before God, we receive our strength. Sometimes God makes us find out the hard way by pulling the rug out from under our feet so that we fall on our faces and look up to Him. Only in my failure did I come to understand that God's grace is sufficient and that His power is made perfect in my weakness.

After finishing my year-long judicial clerkship, I thought I would have clarity on the course for my future. Working for the court gave me insights into the intricacies of the criminal justice system and the people who end up there. As I would talk with the defendants in our courtroom, I learned that none of them had just decided one day to be a criminal. Instead, the roots of their criminal behavior started early in childhood. As I thought about my future, I felt that my best course of action was to pursue a career that focused on children and preventing crime.

As I began to look for a position as a child advocate, I found it difficult to find a position. Despite my experience serving briefly in the juvenile defenders office, I needed more experience to get a job. I started to become discouraged, wondering if this was the path I was really called to take. One afternoon, I had been wrestling with this issue and decided to lie down to take a nap. I fell asleep and began to dream. My dream was the most traumatic dream I had ever experienced. I dreamt about wars, famines and every kind of violence and mayhem imaginable. It was so vivid and uncomfortable, I kept trying to wake myself up. I shook myself out of the dream to the point where I was in a semi-awake state. I found myself having a bit of an out-of-body experience, where I was aware of my surroundings but still in a sleep state. As I lay there, I heard a whisper in my ear that was delivered with such power, it was undeniably the voice of the Holy Spirit. He simply said, "Help the children." I had never experienced anything like and it scared me so much, I jumped from the bed and shook myself completely awake. I paced around the room saying, "I am awake, I am awake."

Those words penetrated so deeply within my spirit. I was no longer confused and knew exactly what I was called to do. It was undeniable. I took the word about children literally and believed that if I was going to make a difference in society, children were the place to start. Only later did God begin to broaden my vision that from His perspective, all the people of the world are children. I once heard author Brennan Manning the Author of "Abbas Child" say, "In heaven there are only five-year-olds." Children learn what they live. Prevention was the best way to achieve this. I was still committed to fighting for reform for adults who are engaged in crime, but believed the most effective course was to strike firmly at the roots. The roots of hate and evil are ingrained in children from the way they are raised.

Even Islamic fundamentalists start teaching Muslim children to hate Christians and Jews from the time they are able to walk. Throughout the Middle East, television shows begin teaching children to become terrorists from very early ages. One show on Hamas television depicts a Mickey Mouse look-alike teaching children to hate and encouraging them to become suicide bombers.

True justice will only occur when societal views and behavior are changed. By focusing my efforts on advocating for policies effecting children, I hoped that lasting change might actually become a reality.

Chapter 9 — Pursuit of Justice

"But let justice roll on like a river, righteousness like a never-failing stream!" — *Amos 5:24 NIV*

Growing up, I had always had a strong heart for justice. It was more of a personal conviction than something I was taught. I often found myself standing up for the "little guy" or intervening on behalf of someone who had been wronged. Justice involves a person getting what he deserves through fair or reasonable treatment. Justice for someone who has been wronged or injured is to see the wrongdoer punished or to receive compensation for the loss. For the wrongdoer, justice would be punishment or penalization for bad behavior.

Among Christians, there are some who align themselves more with the justice side of God, while others align more with His heart of mercy. Of course, both of these principles reflect who God is. He is both just and merciful. Both principles can be found throughout the Bible. Sometimes, I think our tendency is to think of those ideas as mutually exclusive. But I believe both ideas reflect the approach God desires believers to take in dealing with wrongs that have been done to us or to others.

I believed very strongly in the need to see justice done in the Lockerbie bombing. My brother Ken and all the other victims deserved that much. Seeing the people responsible brought to justice also would serve as a deterrent to others who would consider similar acts of terrorism. It would show other would-be terrorists that their behavior is not going to be tolerated and will be severely punished.

Ephesians 6:12 shows the graphic picture of the war being waged in the spiritual realm between good and evil. In some parts of the world, evil seems to dominate and the battle "against the rulers, against the authorities, against the powers of this dark world" is most intense. If we sit silently and do nothing, hate and fear will continue to move forth, unfettered, wreaking havoc on many innocent people's lives. The results of such egregious acts of evil can be found in mass genocides like the Holocaust in Europe in the 1930s and 40s and the atrocities committed in Rwanda in the 1990s.

Micah 6:7 NIV says "O man, what is good; and what does the Lord require of you but to do justice; and to love kindness, and to walk humbly with your God?" Jesus' very own words to the Pharisees in Matthew 23:23 NIV are, "But you have neglected the more important matters of law — justice, mercy and faithfulness." I was determined to do my part to

bring about justice, so I served as my family's chief
advocate and liaison for the Lockerbie criminal trial
itself and the ensuing events that followed.

The Investigation

The investigation into the Lockerbie bombing
began immediately after the bombing itself and has
continued over the course of the last 20 years. It turned
out to be the most expensive criminal investigation
in British history and has involved countless government and law enforcement agencies throughout the
world community. In 1989, the Central Intelligence
Agency concluded that it believed Iran had hired a
Damascus-based radical terrorist organization run
by Ahmed Jibril, called the Popular Front for the
Liberation of Palestine-General Command (PFLP-
GC) to carry out the bombing. The alleged motivation
was in retaliation for the *USS Vincennes'* accidental
shooting down of the Iranian Airbus over the Persian
Gulf in July 1988, which resulted in the deaths of 290
people. Part of the rationale for this belief was that,
in the fall of 1988, a PFLP-GC cell was infiltrated
in Germany. PFLP-GC members were arrested and
several of their bombs seized by West German police.
Because a bomb, planted in a single-speaker Toshiba
radio, was carried out of Germany the day before
the arrest and remained unaccounted for, there was
a belief it may have been the instrument used in the
Lockerbie bombing.[xx] The investigation determined
the Toshiba radio on Pan Am 103 had two speakers
and that the timer was a digital one, set to go off at
a particular time. In contrast, the PFLP-GC bombs

had a sophisticated barometer detonator, equipped with a timer and altimeter that prevented them from exploding before reaching the desired altitude.[xxi] FBI investigators did not find enough evidence to pursue the theory that the PFLP-GC was responsible.

On November 14, 1991, the United States and Britain accused Libyans Abdelbaset Ali Mohmed al-Megrahi and Al-Amin Khalifa Fhimah of involvement in the bombing. Megrahi was a member of the Libyan Intelligence Services, and in particular the head of security of Libyan Arab Airlines, and thereafter the Director of the Center for Strategic Studies in Tripoli, Libya. Fhimah was the former Station Manager of Libyan Arab Airlines in Malta. When Libya refused to turn over the suspects, the U.N. Security Council passed Resolution 748, which compelled Libya to turn over the suspects. Libya's continued refusal resulted in sanctions being imposed on April 15, 1992. These sanctions reduced Libyan diplomatic representation abroad, grounded the national airline and embargoed arms sales.

On November 11, 1993, the U.N. Security Council voted to tighten trade sanctions on Libya to force extradition of the two suspects. The new sanctions included a ban on sales to Libya of equipment for refining and exporting petroleum and a limited freeze on Libyan financial assets overseas. The financial freeze exempted Libyan income from petroleum and agricultural products, the country's only significant exports. In response to the imposition of the new sanctions, Muammar Gaddafi, the leader of Libya, offered to extradite the suspects for a trial in Switzerland. But the United States and its allies insisted on a trial in Scotland.

On December 21, 1994, Libya marked the sixth anniversary of the Lockerbie bombing of Pan Am flight 103 by proposing in a full-page advertisement in the *Washington Post* that the suspects be tried by the Scottish court at the International Court of Justice at the Hague in the Netherlands. The State Department rejected the proposal, and many of the Lockerbie family members were insulted by Gaddafi's approach. For years, he had been trying to get the sanctions lifted through political maneuvering, attempted negotiations and offers to "buy" the Lockerbie family members off with compensation. None of these efforts was acceptable to us. Although I knew the sanctions had to be having adverse effects on the people of Libya more than the government, it was the only course of action to compel Gaddafi to turn the suspects over for trial. We had to remain firm on it.

Growing impatient with the wait, the FBI tried a new tactic to compel Libya to action. They placed the suspects on the *10 Most Wanted List* and offered a $4 million reward for the capture of the suspects. It was touted as the largest reward ever offered in a terrorist case. For the first time in history, the FBI placed information about the fugitives on the Internet and provided an email address where information could be sent. They also instituted a full-blown media campaign in the Middle East and North Africa to use radio, facsimile and matchbook covers in the Arabic language to get the word out.

The years of waiting and hoping continued to take their toll on the families. But Libya continued to hold firm. In June 1997, Libya decided to employ another ridiculous tactic, one I liken to tactics used by domestic abusers who convince their victims to not testify, leaving prosecutors with little case against the abusers. A letter was sent to the Lockerbie families from the United Nations mission in New York in which Libya declared itself ready to enter into serious negotiations about the procedures leading up to the trial. We were most appalled by the letter's allegation that Libya's efforts had not achieved any results because the U.S. government was not really interested in the incident nor really cared about the victims. Libya's agreement to full and immediate cooperation if the United States or Britain would accept any of their previous offers fell on deaf ears because of the manipulative tone with which Libya continued to communicate. Since when do criminals have the ability to negotiate with their victims? The whole thing was morally repugnant and left us more and more disillusioned about the prospect of justice for our loved ones.

Finally, after 10 years of waiting, lobbying and pushing, relief seemed to be in sight. On August 24, 1998, the United States, Britain and the Netherlands announced an unprecedented proposal to convene a Scottish court in the Netherlands to try the Libyans accused of the bombing. The U.N. Security Council backed that decision. A former U.S. Air Force base called Camp Zeist was the proposed location. The base would become temporary Scottish territory and be converted into a court and jail for holding the defendants during their trial. The proposal was designed to meet some of the conditions laid down by Gaddafi for extraditing the two suspects but was coupled with threat of a United Nations' ban on Libya's crude oil export if Libya did not accept the proposal. After pressure from Egyptian President Hosni Mubarek, Libya agreed to the proposal on August 27. But Gaddafi later hesitated on the deal, demanding guarantees that the suspects wouldn't be turned over to Britain. After further encouragement by U.N. Secretary General Kofi Annan and other Middle East leaders, Gaddafi officially told the United Nations that Libya would turn over the two suspects by April 6, 1999.

Gaddafi negotiated the conditions of the suspects' departure and incarceration to the last detail. The chef at the prison was trained how to prepare Libyan food, and Islamic resources and prayer mats were provided. Before they departed, a ceremony was held for Megrahi and Fhimeh with leaders from 40 Middle East and African nations that was likened more to a ceremony for heroes than criminals.

On April 20, 1999, because of Libya's compliance in turning over the suspects for trial, the European Union suspended sanctions against Libya. However, the United States continued to impose sanctions upon the country.

The Trial Begins

After years of false hopes, the suspects appeared before the Scottish court on April 6, 1999, in the

Netherlands and were officially charged with the bombing and murders of 270 victims. It was a day we thought would never come. I felt a small sense of victory just knowing they would finally be tried in a court of law. Due to the unusual nature of this trial, there was little precedent under Scottish law for handling this type of case, so we didn't know what to expect. As both a family member of a victim and an attorney, I had a unique perspective. I was both curious about and whole-heartedly committed to judicial proceedings that were taking place.

I was pleased when a partnership was developed between the U.S. Office of Victims of Crime (OVC) and Syracuse University Law School to host a Web site for the Lockerbie family members where the details of the trial could be posted. The OVC also set up satellite locations where family members could watch the trial proceedings at a couple of locations in New York State and Washington, D.C. Because the trial was being held so far away, it was the only way we could keep up-to-date on what was happening in the trial. That coupled with the occasional article in the British media were the only regular coverage of the case in the news. The U.S. media had all but forgotten the Lockerbie bombing and very few Americans I encountered even knew the trial was going on. That made it difficult when I wanted to talk about the trial or process it with other people, because people just didn't know anything about it. In my heart, I wanted people to care as much about the trial as I did.

Since I was working for an advocacy organization in Washington at the time, I visited the satellite location to watch the trial on several occasions. The OVC also provided funding for each victim's family to send family members a couple times to attend the trial proceedings at Camp Zeist throughout the duration of the trial. I went with my Mom to attend the trial once and another time with my youngest brother, Jason. There was something very significant about sitting in on the trial itself and listening to the case being presented in person. It encouraged me that the case was being taken seriously and prosecuted diligently by the Scottish government.

The courtroom was unique by every standard. It was very modern in appearance, with the most current technological advancements for evidence production and translation. Because of the international nature of the trial, there was simultaneous translation into at least five different languages at any given time. We all had to wear headsets to hear the proceedings. The only things that remotely resembled a traditional British courtroom were the wigs and robes worn by the attorneys and judges.

The proceedings took place behind a giant bullet-proof glass window. There was an intense screening process and identification required for all attendees. The victims' family members sat on the right side of the courtroom and the defendants' families sat on the left. The Libyan defendants wore their finest cultural dress. Seeing their wives in their full Islamic dress and children with them in that courtroom really humanized the defendants in my eyes. I was very curious about them. *What is a family of a terrorist like?* I wanted to go up and talk with them, but we were encouraged not to. Plus, what did I have to say to them? *Hi, my name is Lisa and your husband killed my brother.* It just didn't seem appropriate, so I never did.

Visit to Lockerbie

On the third time I attended the trial, I arranged a stopover in Scotland so I could visit Lockerbie. I had heard many stories from the other Lockerbie families about how their time in Lockerbie impacted them. Since no one in my family had been able to go, I thought it important to the healing process for me to go in person and pass on what I had experienced to the other members of my family.

On the way back from the Netherlands, I flew into Edinburgh and rented a car and drove down to Lockerbie, a town of about 4,000 people in southern Scotland, 80 miles from Edinburgh and 20 miles from the English border. It is primarily an agricultural community with cattle and sheep farming as its main commodity. It was unremarkable by tourist standards. In many ways, though, the Lockerbie tragedy put the town on the map.

It was winter when I visited, and there was a crisp chill in the air. I rented a hotel room at a hotel in downtown Lockerbie. The morning after I arrived, I went to the local public library to do some research. The library was very small, but it included a section dedicated to Lockerbie's history, including the Lockerbie bombing. I sat there for hours, looking through every book and resource available on the village and the tragedy. I wanted to absorb everything I could about its history and the people.

There were photos of the village during World War II, when a POW camp was based there. There were countless photographs of the village following the Lockerbie bombing. Although I had seen many of the photos of the tragedy before, there was something unique about actually looking at those same photos in the place it all happened. It made it all the more real. The photos were horrific views of fire-charred homes and debris scattered throughout 10 square miles of countryside. Sherwood Crescent was the neighborhood hardest hit when the plane's fuel tanks, full of 90 tons of aviation fuel and fuselage, fell on top of a row of six houses, destroying them and leaving a crater in the ground 30 feet deep. The flight deck was found three miles away on top of a hill in the middle of the countryside. The photos reminded me of the pictures I had seen of the devastation that was caused by the atomic bomb that hit Hiroshima during World War II. My senses were on overload.

After leafing through every bit of information I could find, I decided to go out and visit the significant locations of the tragedy. The librarian pointed me in the direction of the places in the village that were important. She encouraged me to end my walk at Drysdale Cemetery, where a garden of remembrance to the victims of Pan Am 103 had been constructed.

It was cold and rainy day, which was typical of Scotland. I felt chilled to my bones as I walked around. Because the village was so small, nothing was really far. The town's cobblestone roads made it look much like what it would have looked like 100 years before. Parts of the village had newer houses and looked like some updating had been done, which was necessary after the damage from the debris of Pam Am Flight 103.

There was a sense of peace there. I found it difficult to imagine the town on the night the plane fell from the sky. It must have been utter chaos. There was also a deep sadness in the spiritual climate of that quaint little village. Sometimes when visiting places where battles have been fought during and where blood has been shed, it is possible to sense the loss of lives in the spirit. I felt that same spirit of grief in Lockerbie, one that ran deep into the heart of the community itself. I found myself connecting with that same spirit and feeling grieved as well. Ken had never visited that place while he was alive and had no personal connection there. But at a heart level, I felt a familial connection to Lockerbie, in ways that few would understand.

There were few visual reminders of the tragedy itself. The crater had been filled and all the buildings that had been destroyed during the bombing were rebuilt by the time I visited. Just stopping at the significant places gave me a bigger perspective on what it was like on that fateful day. After walking around for nearly an hour, I made my way to the most significant memorial. The Drysdale Cemetery, the final resting place of the residents of Lockerbie who lost their lives in the tragedy, was the location of the Garden of Remembrance. The garden was an idyllic place overlooking the Scottish countryside with diverse types of plants interspersed in a circle between individual memorial plaques on the ground, in memory of select Lockerbie family members. There was a large wall memorial dedicated to all the victims killed with the names of each one listed in alphabetical order. With my finger I scanned down the list until I landed on Ken's name. I paused and lingered there for a moment.

For the remainder of history, Ken's name would live on in that place — a place he had never been while he was alive, but nevertheless, a place where he would always be remembered. I found comfort in knowing that he began his journey onto glory from a place like that.

After visiting Lockerbie, I found myself both physically and emotionally tired. So, I went back to my hotel room content with the way I had spent the day. The very next day, I left and drove back to Edinburgh, where I stayed for another two days before flying back to the U.S.

Visiting Lockerbie helped to put the whole tragedy in perspective for me. I felt a connection with that village even though I lived thousands of miles away. The common tragedy we experienced created a heart level connection in the spirit. I felt even more bonded to Scotland because of my Scottish heritage and having attended a Scottish college. The people of the village of Lockerbie were small town people who lived simple lives, but whose lives were turned upside down on December 21, 1988. I was impressed by the care with which the local law enforcement officers had handled the whole investigation, having never experienced anything like this tragedy before. Despite the tremendous death that happened in Lockerbie, it was a peaceful place. It comforted me to know that Ken began his journey to heaven from a place like that.

The Evidence

On May 3, 2000, the trial commenced at the Scottish Court in the Netherlands. The Scottish criminal system has a unique feature that requires that all evidence given at the trial must be corroborated by another source. This provides a more solid foundation in a case, especially in a circumstantial evidence trial.

The Scottish legal procedure that applies to serious criminal charges is called solemn procedure. Ordinarily, a single judge sits with a jury made up of 15 members of the public who are selected at random. However, due to the complexity, anticipated length of the trial and challenge of sequestering jurors from Scotland, a decision was made to have a bench trial with three High Court judges. These judges were charged with hearing the evidence and determining the innocence or guilt of the accused. Lord Sutherland was named as presiding judge, and Lord Coulsfield and Lord MacLean were the other two judges impaneled to serve. A fourth judge, Lord Abernathy was appointed to participate in the deliberations and act as a substitute judge.

A majority decision of the judges is required for any verdict. There are three findings that judges can make when deciding on the guilt or innocence of the accused: guilty, not guilty, or not proven. A not proven verdict is a finding that the burden of proof has not been met by the prosecution. The burden of proof is the same as in the United States, which is proof beyond a reasonable doubt.

Under Scottish law, both the prosecution and defense have a duty to agree to evidence that is not in dispute. Such evidence is put before the court in documents called a "statement of uncontroversial evidence" or a "joint minute of admissions" and is read to the court aloud and becomes part of the evidence. In the Lockerbie trial, there were agreements as to a significant amount of evidence in the trial, especially as it related to the victims killed on the plane. Otherwise, each of the victim's family members would have had to testify that their loved one was on the plane. This would have significantly extended the duration of the trial itself.

The evidence in the trial established that Megrahi and two other Libyan intelligence agents obtained from the Swiss firm Mego AG 40 timers capable of detonating explosive devices. Megrahi worked with Fhimeh to remove luggage tags from Luqa Airport in Malta. On December 7, 1988, Megrahi purchased clothing and an umbrella from a retail store called Mary's House in Sliema, Malta. Megrahi entered Malta using a passport with the alias on December 20, 1988 and stayed at the *Holiday Inn* in Sliema December 20 and 21 under that same alias. A suitcase traveled unaccompanied on an Air Malta flight from Luqa Airport to Frankfurt. In Frankfurt, it was transferred to Pan Am flight 103A, a feeder flight for Pan Am 103. Pan Am 103A carried the suitcase to London's Heathrow Airport, where it was transferred to Pan Am 103 bound for JFK Airport in New York. The suitcase contained the clothing purchased in Malta as well as a Toshiba radio containing an improvised explosive device made of high-performance plastic explosives and programmed to be detonated by electronic timers. The luggage was placed in a luggage container and stored beneath the plane.

The explosive device detonated and exploded onboard the aircraft near Lockerbie. The evidence indicated that the flight left Heathrow Airport late. Had it left on time, the aircraft would have exploded over the ocean, which would have severely hindered the recovery of any evidence.

I was surprised that the prosecution had as much evidence as they did in this case, especially after so many years. Just like putting together pieces in a puzzle, prosecutors were able to develop a picture of what happened. Although they did not have all the pieces, there were enough that you could clearly see what the picture looked like.

The Verdict

On January 31, 2001, eight months after the trial started, the verdicts against the two Libyans were announced. I went to the satellite location in Washington to hear the verdict. There were about 30 people at that remote site. Many of the family members flew to the Netherlands to be there for the verdict. It was an intense time. The OVC provided a trained counselor the Washington D.C. location to serve as a support system for the family members. The room was very quiet and fear permeated the air. People were sitting on the edge of their seats and I could tell that if the decision was not favorable, many of the family members could have serious breakdowns.

As I sat there waiting, I did some self-talk. As I processed the way I was feeling, I felt God's peace upon me. I knew that no matter what happened I would be okay. God had already done enough healing in my heart that my personal well-being was not tied to the outcome of the trial.

The first accused, Megrahi, was found guilty of murder by a unanimous verdict. The second accused, Fhimah, was found not guilty by a unanimous verdict. Megrahi received a mandatory sentence of life imprisonment with no opportunity to be considered for parole until he had served a minimum of 20 years.

Five days later, Libyan leader Muammar Gaddafi declared Libya's innocence and accused U.S. investigators of manipulating evidence. Megrahi filed an appeal of his conviction and on March 14, 2002, his appeal was denied and his murder conviction was upheld.

I was very happy when Megrahi was convicted of the Lockerbie bombing. I felt like all our persistence had paid off and justice was finally served. Most of the family members believed Gaddafi himself ordered the bombing. But we realized we would never see him charged criminally. There just wasn't enough evidence to charge him directly. So the best we could hope for was a civil judgment against Libya and an acceptance of responsibility for the bombing. That was the next step in the process, and our civil attorneys were hard at work preparing our case.

Only then would reconciliation with Libya be possible.

Chapter 10 — The Biblical Response

"But to you who are willing to listen, I say, love your enemies! Do good to those who hate you. Bless those who curse you. Pray for those who hurt you." — Luke 6:27-28 NLT

In December 1999, I moved from Omaha, Nebraska to Washington D.C. to start a new job with a national advocacy organization. After taking the Georgia bar exam, I had planned to move to Georgia to make a new start. But, God completely redirected my path and took me to Omaha to participate in a year-long urban missions program with Lutheran Service Corps. I lived in an intentional Christian community and worked for social justice as a full-time volunteer with a state-wide child advocacy organization. After my year was finished, I was hired on full-time as the Director of Policy. I continued in that position for another two years, before moving to

Washington D.C. to work as State Operations Director for an organization of law enforcement officers that advocate for strategies that keep kids from getting involved in crime.

I also started attending Mclean Bible Church in Mclean, Virginia. The church had a dynamic Generation X ministry called Frontline that met Sunday evenings. The group's emphasis was on life change through biblical community. But it also had a strong commitment to local outreach and global missions. This church sent out about 20 short-term teams a year just from within the Frontline community and a few others from the larger church body. Before making the move to the D.C. area, God had begun to stir in my heart the desire to be involved in international missions. So I was really excited for the opportunity to be a part of a community that was involved in missions.

The first year I was working in Washington, I was responsible for launching and supervising the existing and new state offices for our association of law enforcement professionals that advocated for strategies to keep kids from getting involved in crime. I traveled throughout the country to different law enforcement association meetings and to interface with our state office directors. This busy travel schedule prevented me from being involved in any missions for all of 2000.

About this same time, God was beginning to challenge my perspective on how I should be responding to Muslims from a biblical perspective. When you lose a loved one as a result of Islamic terrorism, the

tendency is to lump all Muslims into the same cate-
gory and demonize an entire group of people. God
began to challenge me that although seeking justice
in the Lockerbie bombing was important, He wanted
me to take it further.

As a believer, I knew it was wrong to hate. Even
hating someone who did something horrendous to
you or someone you loved was wrong. For years, I
resolved myself to being indifferent to Muslims. I
didn't really know any Muslims and that was the way
I wanted to keep it. But then God began to challenge
me on what His word says about loving my enemies.
He brought me to Scriptures like Matthew 5:43 and
Luke 6:27. Matthew 5:43 NLT says, "You have heard
that the law of Moses says 'Love your neighbor and
hate your enemy.' But I say love your enemies! Pray
for those who persecute you! In that way, you will be
acting as true children of your Father in heaven. For
He gives His sunlight to both the evil and the good,
and He sends rain on the just and on the unjust too. If
you love only those who love you, what good is that?
Even corrupt tax collectors do that much. If you are
kind only to your friends, how are you different from
anyone else? Even pagans do that. But you are to be
perfect, even as your Father in heaven is perfect."

As I read the word, I was confronted with the
reality that, as a follower of Christ, I was expected to
behave in a way that was different than everyone else.
It was counter-cultural. But then the very foundation
of the gospel of Jesus Christ is counter-cultural. Many
of the Lockerbie family members were crippled with
anger and bitterness toward Libyans. I did not feel

that way. It was not enough for me to just not hate Libyans or Muslims. I was called to love Muslims. I was challenged about how I could love a group of people I didn't even know. In my heart, I knew that absent the Holy Spirit's power in my life, I could not love them. So, from that day forth, I began to embark on my journey of learning who the Muslim people are and how to love them.

One of the foundational ways we are called to love our enemies is to forgive them. The very definition of forgiveness is about canceling the debt someone owes. The Word of God has a lot to say about forgiveness. Because we have been forgiven of our sins, we must forgive others. The focus of the Christian faith is about loving God and my neighbor. They cannot be separated. So what I do on the horizontal in my relationships with other people, tells God what I think of Him.

At times in Christian circles, we throw the idea of forgiveness at people who have been seriously wronged in a way that says, "What happened to you doesn't matter. You just need to get over it and forgive." From a Western viewpoint, forgiveness is often seen through a unilateral lens. Forgiveness is simply about letting go of the wrong so we feel better. In our efforts to keep people from succumbing to bitterness, we severely minimize the pain that those who have been sinned against feel.

I serve a God who cares deeply for the brokenhearted and the victimized. If He did not connect with the brokenness of people, He would seem apathetic. We live in a present evil age where countless wrongs like abuse, oppression, terrorism and persecution are perpetrated against innocent people daily. Why would anyone want to be in relationship with a God who cares so little about the wrongs that have been done to them?

God is both just and forgiving. Romans 12:19 NLT says, "Dear friends, never take revenge yourselves. Leave that to the righteous anger of God. For the Scriptures say 'I will take revenge, I will pay them back,' says the Lord." To avenge is to give justice to someone who has been wronged. While in Exodus 34:6-7 NIV the Lord said, "The LORD, the LORD, the compassionate and gracious God, slow to anger, abounding in love and faithfulness, 7 maintaining love to thousands, and forgiving wickedness, rebellion and sin. Yet he does not leave the guilty unpunished; he punishes the children and their children for the sin of the fathers to the third and fourth generation." Yet we are all sinners and have been sinned against at the same time. When Christ died on the cross for our sins, He gave us the ability through His blood shed on the cross to be forgiven. 1 John 1:9 ESV says, "If we confess our sins, he is faithful and just to forgive our sins and cleanse us from all unrighteousness."

One of the conditions of our being forgiven by God is that we confess and repent of our sins. When we confess our sins, God promises to forgive and to never again remember them. Yet sometimes we read Scripture in such a way as to skip the requirement of repentance from the person who wronged us in order for forgiveness to occur. I believe this seriously undermines the bilateral motivation of forgiveness, which is to be a catalyst to reconciliation.

Because the Christian walk is primarily about relationship, the motivation of forgiveness is to see relationships healed and restored. When I am wronged, the call to forgive relates both to my relationship with God and the wrongdoer. Colossians 3:13 NLT says, "Make allowance for each other's faults, and forgive the person who offends you. Remember the Lord forgave you, so you must forgive others." (see also Ephesians 4:32) There is the presumption that as fallible humans, we will do things to hurt one another. When we wrong one another, there is an expectation that the person who has been wronged will confront the wrongdoer and give him an opportunity to confess and repent. Only when they repent can reconciliation be pursued.

At times, the person who has wronged you does not confess their sin or repent of their wrongdoing. Or in other situations, the wrongdoer's repentance is not heartfelt because it doesn't include a change in behavior. In those cases, true forgiveness cannot happen. The injured person ends up being bound in inner turmoil as he or she continues to litigate their case in the internal courtroom of their heart. The incident gets replayed over and over again. The result is many hurting people get bound in pain-numbing behaviors that can keep their pain buried deep beneath the surface. Even believers, who are told by well-meaning fellow Christians to just forgive, can't seem to find freedom.

Perhaps because we are humans created in God's image, justice is ingrained in who we are. As people who are injured, we long for our day in court and to see our wrong made right. In order to keep from becoming bound in bitterness or despair, we release those sins to God to be litigated in heaven's court-room. Releasing our wrong to God and trusting in His justice brings the freedom in our hearts so that our prayers are not hindered, as is talked about in Mark 11:25. We can claim the promise that "The Lord will fight for you, you need only be still." (Exodus 14:14 NIV) We can trust that the Lord, who has made Himself the advocate, judge, and the jury will surely bring justice and right the wrong.

Personal Forgiveness

Soon after Megrahi was convicted of the Pan Am 103 bombing the Lord put it on my heart to send him a letter in prison. Up to that point, he still maintained his innocence for the bombing. In the letter, I shared about my brother and my faith and that as a follower of Christ I needed to forgive him. In it, I confessed that only God knew if he was really responsible but that I had to release my offense against him as Mark 11:25 talked about. He wrote a very kind letter back to me assuring me of his innocence and good nature. His letter included a quote from the Qur'an and Luke 18 from the Bible. Despite his continued claim of innocence, I had done what I needed to free up my heart. Knowing that forgiveness was not an Islamic concept, I hoped that through my simple act of obedience, maybe the light of Christ had shone into Megrahi's heart.

During this journey of learning the biblical response to terrorism, Romans 12:21 became a prophetic Scripture for my brother's death and how God wanted me to respond. Even the chapter and verse have significance, since Ken's death was on 12-21-88. Romans 12:21 NLT says "Don't let evil conquer you, but conquer evil by doing good." Since I believe that nothing happens by chance, when there is a wrong done to us, God desires for us to find a way to see that wrong redeemed for His glory. Romans 12:20 NLT gives some sound advice on how to do that, "If your enemies are hungry, feed them. If they are thirsty, give them something to drink. In doing this, you will heap burning coals of shame on their heads." Only in the upside down nature of the Kingdom of God would it ever make sense to respond to hate with love. But because God's ultimate purpose is redemption of all mankind, including His lost children of Islam, then it makes absolute sense. Although I still didn't fully understand how it was all going to play out yet, I knew that if I was going to play a part in overcoming the evil of terrorism, the weapon I needed to use was the weapon of love.

It is one thing to talk about loving your enemies intellectually, and a very different thing to walk it out. As I began to explore the idea of reaching out to Muslims, I found myself a bit resistant. At the center of Islamic terrorism is fear for the purpose of gaining control. I was struggling with fear about getting involved in outreach to Muslims. What would they think of me? How would they respond? Would they want to harm me as well? These were the kinds of questions I was wrestling with.

"There is no fear in love. But perfect love drives out all fear, because fear has to do with punishment. The one who fears is not made perfect in love." (1 John 4:18 NIV) I knew that the only way my fear would go away was for me to press through the fear as I allowed God to show me His heart for the Muslim people.

Preparing To Go

In February 2001, I saw a posting at church for a mission trip to Egypt. From the moment I saw the posting, I knew I was supposed to go. I had always been fascinated with Egyptian history, but I was also interested in the nature of the trip. Egypt is known as the intellectual center of Islam, while Saudi Arabia is seen as the spiritual center. Our team was composed of all leaders. Each of us was serving in formal leadership positions in our jobs or in ministry. We were to be focusing on building bridges with Egyptian leaders and working with the poorest of the poor in Egypt. I knew it would be a perfect place for my first involvement in Muslim outreach.

I was accepted on the team, and in April we began regular team meetings. Global Impact, the mission's ministry within my church, had a policy of requiring team members to go through six months of training, team building and fundraising activities together. From the beginning, our team hit it off. Because we were all strong leaders, the challenge was to keep us from all trying to lead the team because we already had two capable team leaders. We really were a strong, tight-knit community, each with a common desire to really learn about Islam and how to minister to the Muslim people. For six months, we read several books on Islam, visited local Middle East restaurants, met with Islamic leaders at a local mosque and prayed through the streets of Muslim neighborhoods. Through that process, God really began to open my eyes and heart to the Muslim people and their unique worldview and culture. When early September came around, we were making the last push to raise funds for our team and preparing to leave for Egypt in early October 2001.

But our plans were about to come to a screeching halt.

Chapter 11 — Terrorism Becomes A Household Word

"Deliver me from my enemies, O my God: protect me from those who rise up against me; deliver me from those who work evil, and save me from bloodthirsty men." — Psalms 59:1,2 ESV

On September 11, 2001, I was attending a conference of the National Governor's Association on early childhood education at the Watergate Hotel in Washington, D.C. As was typical, I made the commute into the city from my home in Northern Virginia by way of the Virginia Railway Express. However, instead of making the transfer to the Red Line Metrorail at Union Station and traveling up to Dupont Circle, I transferred at L'Enfant Plaza and took the Blue Line to Foggy Bottom Station. From there I walked over to the Watergate Hotel, which was located directly across the Potomac

River from the Pentagon and a block from the State Department. It was a typical fall day in Washington D.C. The weather was still pretty warm and there was a bit of humidity in the air. The leaves on the trees were just beginning to change colors.

At 8:30 a.m., the director of the National Governor's Association Early Childhood Project prepared to open the meeting. Governor Michael Easley of North Carolina was scheduled to be our keynote speaker and the lead speaker that morning. When the early childhood director approached the microphone, she was obviously shaken. Rather than introducing Governor Beasley, she announced the news of the first plane flying into the World Trade Center. It was clear that although the details and motivation were still sketchy, there must have been a presumption of wrong doing, because she said that they were evacuating the governors and the conference was canceled. She told us there were television sets in the lobby of the hotel that we could watch.

I was completely caught off-guard. Not knowing what else to do, I headed upstairs to the lobby of the hotel so I could find out more details about the World Trade Center. The newscasters were giving a play-by-play of the unfolding events. New York City was in complete chaos. About 20 of us sat in the lobby of the hotel, glued to the television. We were almost spellbound when we watched the second plane fly into the World Trade Center. The live broadcast of the developments in New York were interrupted with news of the another plane that just crashed into the Pentagon. I found myself almost incapacitated as

I sat there watching the screen. I could not believe my eyes. A few moments later, two women from the conference came down from their hotel room and announced that they could see the Pentagon and it was on fire, with smoke billowing out over the Potomac River.

At this point, people started to scramble to get out of town. We could sense that things weren't over yet. Because I took the commuter train in from Virginia, it only ran in the mornings and the evenings after work. So, I didn't really have a good way to get out of town. At best, I could take the Blue Line of the Metrorail to the last station in Springfield, Virginia. It was only 15 minutes from my house. If I could get there, maybe I could get a ride from my roommate or take a taxi to my condo in Lorton. Just then, the front desk clerk of the hotel came over to announce that all the Metrorails had been shut down for security concerns. All I could do was sit there and wait. I felt like a sitting duck. Just then, the news reported the Capitol was being evacuated, as well as other government buildings. There was believed to be another plane heading for Capitol Hill. Then another reporter broke in with a report that they believed a car bomb had just exploded outside the State Department. *The State Department? That's a block from here,* I thought. I started to tremble with fear.

People in the hotel lobby were all trying to make phone calls out, but the circuits were all jammed. I decided to try my cell phone as well, hoping maybe I would be the lucky one. I knew my family would be worried when they heard the news. But, no luck.

I couldn't get through either. Some people just sat blind-eyed with tears, and others were scrambling. Several people were able to get reservations for rental cars and were determined to get out of town as soon as possible. They grabbed their suitcases and bolted out the door.

It seemed like time was standing still. We didn't know what else to do but to sit there and pray silently as we watched the news. The images of people jumping to their deaths out of the windows of the World Trade Center was the most disturbing thing I had ever seen. Emergency crews were on the scene at both the World Trade Center and the Pentagon. Then if things couldn't get any worse, we watched as the Twin Towers of the World Trade Center crumbled to the ground. I had never seen anything like it. For the first time, I began to wonder whether I was going to make it out of the city alive.

There was a priest from a local Catholic Church attending the conference. He was going from person to person in the lobby, seeing if he could do anything to comfort them. Then he stood up and made an announcement. "Excuse me, I feel like at a time like this, it would be good if we could get together and pray. If you are interested, join me over in the corner."

I jumped up and swiftly walked over to the corner. *Absolutely, prayer is the best idea yet. God is our ever-present help in time of need.* About eight of us gathered in a circle to pray. We seemed to be a group of people from a variety of different ethnic and religious backgrounds, but at a time like that, differences seemed insignificant. The priest led with the first prayer. We needed to receive God's grace in that moment more than anything else. We still didn't know who was responsible, but in our hearts we knew that our nation was being attacked. I knew in my spirit that it was Islamic terrorists. Some of the people in our prayer group spoke their own prayers and others just sat silently in agreement.

With the city of Washington so dependent on public transportation, there was a whole city full of stranded commuters. Law enforcement personnel were sent into the Metro stations to secure a limited number of them so commuters could get out of the city and back home. At about 3 p.m. that day, I walked over to the Foggy Bottom Metro station to catch a train home. The streets were nearly empty. It reminded me of a scene out of an apocalyptic movie. Frankly, I was scared to death to even enter the Metro station, but I had no choice. I had to risk it. Commuters on the Metro were more stoic than usual. All the passengers seemed to be in their own world, processing the events of the day, but dumbfounded with what to say.

When I arrived at Springfield Metro Station, it was chaotic, with people scrambling to catch buses or taxis home. The Springfield Police Department was on hand to regulate things and keep people calm. By then, the cell towers were clear and I was able to get through to my roommate Lynne to come pick me up.

Ministering To Others

The following day, I felt traumatized by the events. It was clear that it was an orchestrated act of terrorism. Joni Erickson Tada, a well-known Christian author and speaker, volunteered to come to my church in Mclean, Virginia to offer some encouragement to people who were struggling with God's perspective on what happened and to pray together. There were several people from my church who were at the Pentagon when the plane crashed into the building. One soldier shared his story about how he and several of his co-workers had decided to go to the cafeteria for a donut. As they were about to leave the office, that soldier's wife called him, so he sent his co-workers on without him. That call saved his life. Minutes later, the plane flew into the Pentagon, completely destroying the cafeteria and killing all his co-workers. By God's grace, his life was spared.

Joni Erickson Tada spoke to our congregation on the issue of suffering. It is a topic that few talk about within the church, but as a quadriplegic person who works with disabled people, she is familiar with the topic. Her approach was sobering. Rather than focusing on "why God allowed it," she challenged us to think about the power of prayer and how God is acting to protect us and keep bad things from happening. So often we focus on the bad things, instead of how God co-labors with us through our prayers to prevent more evil acts from happening. I felt challenged on my perspective.

Once again, I had been directly impacted by terrorism. But rather than shrink back in fear, the missions team scheduled to go to Egypt was more determined than ever to go. What better time to go to the Muslim people and respond in love toward them? One teammate was an FBI agent assigned to investigate the wreckage of the Pentagon. It quickly became clear that he and a couple of our other team members who worked in security-related positions with the U.S. government would likely not be able to go on the trip.

Then word got out to the general congregation about our mission trip, and people put pressure on our senior pastor not to let us go. People were concerned about our safety in Egypt from other militant Islamists. I felt like we were playing into the enemy's hands by letting fear keep us from going. In the end, despite our best wishes, the trip was canceled.

I was left with a void in my heart. I could not understand how after six months of preparation and God opening my heart to serve the Muslim people, our trip was canceled. It seemed like it was all for nothing. Or so I thought. But in the months that followed, I began to understand that sometimes, God can use *not* going on a mission trip as much as going on a mission trip to develop a heart for the Muslim people. I knew that the next mission opportunity to go the Muslim world that presented itself, I would be a part of it.

The terrorist attacks of September 11 were the biggest attack on U.S. soil since the bombing of Pearl Harbor 60 years earlier. The difference was that it was an attack directed at innocent people rather than military targets. For the first time, war on terrorism became a household phrase. It was a senseless act of violence that left an entire nation reeling.

Since I had been engaging in the war on terrorism for more than 12 years, I had a unique perspective on the issue. I was able to provide words of encouragement for those who were grieving and offered a listening ear to victims who had lost people in the attack. Many people were struggling. A woman on my softball team who was a flight attendant was struggling with both guilt and relief, because she was originally scheduled to be on the United Airlines flight that was flown into the Pentagon, but she called in sick. She felt blessed to be alive, but grieved for the flight attendants who died. It was a lot for anyone to handle.

Another woman from my church was significantly traumatized. She worked at an office across the street from the Pentagon and actually looked out her window to see the look of fear on the faces of the passengers of the United flight seconds before it slammed into the Pentagon. The looks on their faces seemed to be burned in her mind, making it difficult to move on.

Because I had suffered a similar loss, I was able to encourage others. I was also able to serve as a voice of reason for those who wanted to repay hate with hate. Rather than preaching at people, I simply shared my story of how God had moved in my life to take me from death to life again. Sometimes, it seemed that people just needed to know that what they were feeling was normal, and that one day, they would be able to move on.

On A Mission

While the rest of the world was still struggling to come to terms with September 11 and how to most effectively wage the war on terrorism, I began my own mission. I was more convinced than ever that the war that was being waged was a spiritual one. Terrorism would continue to spread throughout the world as the enemy sought to destroy the Kingdom of God. As a member of that kingdom, I had to take seriously the call to be involved in the Great Commission. I was called to be an ambassador of reconciliation. I allowed that call to penetrate deep within my being. The Apostle Paul in 2 Corinthians refers to this passionate commitment to the ministry of reconciliation as being seen as craziness by others. Christ's love compels us to be involved in the ministry of reconciliation. For Christ's love compels us, because we are convinced that one died for all, and therefore all died. And he died for all, that those who live should no longer live for themselves but for him who died for them and was raised again. (2 Corinthians 5:14-15 NIV) As I grew in my understanding for God's heart and love for His lost children, I took seriously the call to be involved in being His ambassador.

The desire to go to the nations and be Christ's ambassador was a nearly all-consuming flame that had been lit within my heart. I guess when you experience the fragility of life on more than one occasion, you really understand life is short. I knew I had to make it count. The first opportunity that presented itself to go on a medical mission trip in 2002 was a trip to Kenya. I had always wanted to go to Africa, and the opportunity to serve the poorest of the poor in Africa, who had no access to medical care, would be a privilege. That trip taught me much about suffering and the need for childlike faith. I was humbled by the amount of faith that the Kenyan people have in believing that prayer could heal them as effectively as medical treatment could. Despite the desperate poverty and suffering we saw, God appeared bigger to me there than He ever had.

Immediately upon returning from Kenya, I signed up for another mission trip to Indonesia in January 2003. I was so excited about the opportunity to go to the largest Muslim country in the world. We would spend half of our two and a half weeks in a town in the northernmost tip of Sumatra, called Banda Aceh, and the other half of our time was in Java. We flew into Bali, then took a 15-minute flight on a small plane to an island off Bali called Lombok.

Banda Aceh was considered the most strict Islamic region in Indonesia, because the people were under Shari'a law. The people had been engaged in a civil war against the Indonesian government for many years and had just entered a cease-fire agreement and were under marshal law. We saw the hands of God in it and knew that He was opening a door for us to go into a region where few had been able to go.

A month before we were set to leave for Indonesia, terrorists bombed a hotel in Bali, killing several tourists. I couldn't imagine the possibility of my trip being canceled again because of terrorism. I was more determined than ever to go. None of our team members seemed the least bit apprehensive about going, either. Thankfully, our church leadership supported our decision to still go.

Our time in Indonesia was spent building friendships with the Indonesians and helping at a local English club. I was especially shocked at how friendly the Acehnese people were to us. They seemed very religiously devout and were very diligent about following Islamic law. So many people throughout Indonesia seemed scared of the Acehnese and couldn't believe we would go there. When we met new friends, they would always offer their condolences for September 11th and ask us if we were afraid to come to Indonesia because of the Bali bombing. It provided a natural bridge to share about my brother's death by terrorism and about how my faith had brought me through. It also allowed me to share that out of that tragedy, I wanted to come and meet Muslims and see what they were really like. It was the first time I really began to understand the power and redemptive purposes that God can use in a tragedy like my brother's death.

When I went to Indonesia, I knew that I still did not have the ability to love the Muslim people in my own strength. Even realizing that all Muslims aren't terrorists and many condemn that acts of terror carried out by the Islamic fundamentalists, I was still apprehensive because of all that I had seen and experienced at the hands of terrorists. I asked God to show me His heart for the Muslim people and the way He viewed them. One day while we were in Aceh, we went out in groups of two for a prayer walk, an envisioning activity where you walk through the streets and neighborhoods and allow God to speak to you and show you who the people really are, so you can more effectively intercede for them. My teammate, Elyse Bauer and I walked the streets and prayed together one morning. I was overcome by the sights, sounds and smells — the odor of trash burning in a nearby alley, the aroma of fresh bread from a small bakery, the sound of shopkeepers sweeping the walkways of their shops, the sight of women busying themselves with their laundry. As we approached the ladies, we smiled and greeted them in the Indonesian language.

When we were nearing the end of our prayer walk, we approached a yard with children playing in it. There must have been five of them of all different ages and sizes. As we paused to pray, I heard God speak to my heart "This is how I see them! They are my lost children whom I dearly love and I am desperate to have them back in relationship with me!" I started to weep, because in that moment I could feel the heart of God yearning for His children to come home. Yet, they don't know Him. Instead, they are caught up in religious practice, all the while trying to earn God's favor when He desires to offer it to them freely.

Rather than feeling despair, I felt hope. After all, the gospel of Jesus Christ really is good news and I had the opportunity to be a part of extending God's hand of grace to His lost children. In that moment, I got just a glimpse of how my being involved in reconciling people to Jesus could also play a role in reconciling nations.

Chapter 12 — Redemptive Suffering

"Praise be to the God and Father of our Lord Jesus Christ, the Father of compassion and the God of all comfort, who comforts us in all our troubles, so that we can comfort those in any trouble with the comfort we ourselves received from God." — *2 Corinthians 1:3-4 NIV*

The way of the cross is the way of suffering. Yet in many Christian circles, people believe that suffering is punishment for sin rather than a pathway to the resurrection power of Christ. The natural human tendency is to eliminate all forms of suffering from our life. But suffering in some form or another is the product of our lives as human beings.

I have found that the way we respond to that suffering can either send us spiraling into the pit of despair or bring us closer to God. Our suffering also can cause us to look at the world in a whole new way and use that suffering for God's redemptive purposes.

Suffering can come in many different forms — physical pain, mental anguish, poverty, sickness, depression, delays, loneliness, the death of a loved one. Of course we serve a God who still answers prayer, and He calls us to bring our hurts and needs to the throne of grace and ask for relief. At times, our relief is not immediate or we do not see it at all. This can leave us confused or disillusioned with the ways of God or His heart for us.

In my life, I have had many struggles. Physical illness has been a source of much pain and suffering. Even to this day, I experience daily joint and muscle pain from my lupus. As I am working on this book, I am suffering with a painful case of shingles, which causes severe nerve pain, and a rash along one side of the body. I have received prayer for healing and I continue to believe for that to happen, but as of now I still wait. Rather than letting these sufferings I experience in my life disable me, I try to daily embrace them and follow hard after God in the midst of them.

The Way Of The Cross

The way of the cross is about dying to self so that we might have greater life through Christ. In my life, the death of my brother caused great turmoil and pain to me and my family. But it also proved the perfect example of the cost of following Christ. It was a hate-filled act of terrorism directed at Americans and at

Christians because the world sees the United States as a Christian nation. The cost of the cross in my brother's death was not only losing someone I dearly loved, but also dying to my selfish desire to hold back forgiveness and allowing bitterness to fill my heart. As Jesus hung on the cross with blood dripping from his broken body, He spoke words of life on behalf of the very people who caused His death. These simple words He uttered, "Forgive them, Father, for they know not what they do," had eternal significance that transcended time.

It is almost unfathomable to think about. At times, our tendency is to rationalize Jesus' behavior based on the fact that He was God. Of course, He could do that. But, we are simple humans who couldn't possibly do such a thing. Yet, it is that very thing God is calling us to do.

Experiencing suffering tests our faith and produces perseverance. James 1:2 NIV says "Consider it pure joy, my brothers, when you face trials of many kinds, because you know that testing of your faith develops perseverance. Perseverance must finish its work so then you may be mature and complete, not lacking anything."

In the process of mining diamonds or gold, miners use dynamite to blast into the caverns where the stones can be found to produce diamonds. God often allows a blast in our lives to bring forth the precious jewels he originally designed us to be.

Like the fire used to purify gold, God also uses His refining fire to produce the shining gold in us. Sometimes the trials we suffer are designed to purify us. These trials are only to test our faith, to show that it is strong and pure. It is being tested as fire tests and purifies gold — and our faith is more precious to God than mere gold.

Suffering is not only a natural part of the human life, it is essential for the Christian life. We are invited to accompany Jesus on His journey. That choice includes the road of suffering. Jesus calls followers of Christ to join Him in His suffering in Mark 8:34 NIV, "If anyone would come after me, he must deny himself and take up his cross and follow me. For whoever wants to save his life will lose it, but whoever loses his life for me and the gospels will save it." So, as we identify with Christ and lose our life for the gospel, we preserve our life. Through embracing suffering and death, we gain new life. But we can't do it on our own. It requires us to renounce reliance on any and every human resource and to throw ourselves onto the throne of God's grace and acknowledge our utter dependence on Him for everything.

At times in my life, I believed that there were areas of my life I needed God's help to make it through, and others I could handle myself. Through losing my brother and the ensuing havoc it caused in my life, I came to the end of myself. In ancient times when it became evident that a warrior in a sword fight was going to lose the battle, he would fall on his sword, taking his own life. In our lives as believers, God is beckoning us to fall on our swords and trust that He will bring us new life. Exodus 14:14 NIV says, "The Lord will fight for you; need only be still."

The way of the gospel is counter-cultural. It was through Christ's death on the cross that we can have eternal life. There is nothing more important to God than redeeming His long-lost children. Knowing that a sacrifice had to be made, He made the eternal sacrifice of His own life. It was an incredibly difficult and painful sacrifice. He experienced every temptation imaginable so He could identify with what we as humans go through, yet was without sin. Then He was betrayed by one of His closest friends and then denied by another. He was wrongfully charged, mocked, beaten and spit upon. Were that not enough, He was forced to carry the heavy cross along the grueling path to Calvary. Only when His body crumbled from the sheer weight of the cross was someone commissioned to help Him. Luke 23:26 ESV gives the account, "As they led Jesus away, a man named Simon, who was from Cyrene, happened to be coming in from the countryside. The soldiers seized him and put the cross on him and made him carry it behind Jesus."

There was no willing volunteer to help Jesus carry the cross. Instead Simon, a man from what is now modern day Libya, was given the responsibility to help carry the burden.

It should have been a privilege to carry the cross for Jesus Christ, the Savior of the world. Where were all His followers then, at the time of His lowest moment and greatest need? None of His closest friends stepped in to intervene. Instead, He died alone on Calvary next to criminals, while onlookers jeered at him and gambled for the remains of His clothing.

It was the most humiliating experience any person could imagine, especially for an innocent man.

Yet, He did it for us, His children whom He dearly loves. What He asks in return is that we deny ourselves and take up our cross and follow Him. He doesn't want to force us like Simon of Cyrene was. Instead, He wants our motivation to be sacrificial love for Him — like the love He gave us.

In the Garden of Eden there was suffering. Suffering came from the enemy and is a result of the fall. However, God's solution to the problem of suffering was not to eliminate it completely or insulate us from it. Instead, God's solution to the problem of suffering is to take it on with full force and then transform it into the redemption of mankind. The Apostle Paul models this principle in Philippians 3:8-11 ESV, "For His sake I have suffered the loss of all things and count them as rubbish, in order that I may gain Christ and be found in Him, not having a righteousness of my own that comes from the law, but that which comes from faith in Christ, the righteousness from God that depends on faith — that I may know Him and the power of his resurrection and may share His sufferings, becoming like Him in His death, that by any means possible, I may attain the resurrection from the dead."

The early church completely embraced redemptive suffering. They embraced the fact that they were weak and that God's light and power were held in "perishable containers" so that everyone would see that their power was from God and not their own. (2 Corinthians 4:7 NLT) 2 Corinthians 4:8 says, "We are pressed on every side by troubles, but we are not crushed. We are perplexed, but not driven to despair. We are hunted down, but never abandoned by God. We get knocked down, but we are not destroyed. Through suffering our bodies continue to share in the death of Jesus so that the life of Jesus may also be seen in our bodies." The early church and much of the church around the world today also has face persecution that makes my sufferings pale in comparison. "Yes, we live under constant danger of death because we serve Jesus, so that the life of Jesus will be obvious in our dying bodies. So we live in the face of death, but it has resulted in eternal life for you."(2 Corinthians 4:11-12 NLT) In the process of suffering and dying to self, they became more dependent upon Christ and thereby radiated more of His glory in the midst of their trials. As they took on death, it resulted in eternal life for people who did not know Christ. That was the redemptive purpose behind it. Even though times were hard, they continued to preach the word and believe God would use them to bring more and more people to Christ and give God more and more glory. They trusted God to one day raise them up just as He did Jesus Christ.

Revelation 12:11 NIV says "They overcame him by the blood of the Lamb and by the word of their testimony; they did not love their lives so much as to shrink from death." This verse shows a perfect illustration of the power of suffering in overcoming the enemy. The blood of the Lamb is a symbol of sacrifice and death and the word of the testimony is the story of how God uses death to bring life. Through our sufferings and dying to self, God can take our story, if we let Him, and use it to testify to His redeeming power in our lives. We can encourage others in their sufferings as well as drawing others to the power of Christ in us, in the midst of our sufferings. It is a powerful testimony and one that can stop the enemy dead in his tracks.

God does not ask us to go the way of suffering simply because Jesus did. It is not something good in itself. At the cross, God took a terrible tragedy and turned it into triumph. At the cross, God took loss and failure and turned it into a new dependence on Him. On that same cross, God took my brother's murder and my own chronic joint pain and gave me a heartfelt compassion for others who are suffering. God uses suffering because suffering and death are signs of human weakness and defeat. In our weakness and defeat, God is strong.

Recently, I attended the Saturday night service at my church during the Palm Sunday weekend. The topic of the sermon was on redemptive suffering. The Easter season has always been the best time to reflect on Jesus' death and the fierce suffering that accompanied it. Sometimes, our tendency in the church is to quickly glaze over the death part of Jesus' life so we can get to His resurrection. The death is the painful part, so we don't want to stay there. Especially as Western Christians, suffering is uncomfortable and we don't want to embrace it. Instead, we want to move on to the joyous part — the resurrection. Of course, the resurrection is the most important part. That is where Jesus is most glorified. But what about in His death? Was Jesus also glorified in His death and suffering? I believe He was. Because without the death, there could be no resurrection. With death, comes life.

The *Passion of the Christ* movie did an excellent job of portraying the immense pain that Christ suffered at the hands of the Roman soldiers. That visual depiction was more horrific than I had ever imagined. He was tortured in virtually every way imaginable. Although it was difficult to watch Jesus suffer like that, it gave me a deeper appreciation of how painful it really was for Him. Jesus could have lessened the pain or ended it completely. But He refused to go that route. Instead, he embraced it fully, knowing that was the only way for our redemption.

As I sat in the Easter service at my church, a picture entered my mind of a little girl at Calvary on the day that Jesus died. Rather than hiding like many of Jesus' disciples did, she climbed the hill that Jesus' cross stood upon. She wrapped her arms around the cross and embraced it like she was holding on for her life. As she embraced the cross, drops of Jesus' blood fell from His torn body onto her forehead. I heard the words: "There is safety and security in the cross." In that moment, I realized that little girl was me and God was calling me to not just endure the suffering, but to embrace it like He did. By embracing the death, I would see more life and power on the other side of the suffering.

We embrace suffering as well for the spiritual growth it entails. For when we are weak, we are strong. (2 Corinthians 12:10) For when we are weak,

God's spirit working in and through us empowers us to press through the suffering to the redemptive purpose on the other side.

Through the suffering I have experienced in my life, I have gained a deeper awareness of the suffering of society as a whole. Terrorism, oppression, poverty, disease and persecution are only a few of the societal evils that plague nations around the world. God uses us as His hands and feet to extend His resurrection power through redemption to mankind. In my life, God has used my suffering to identify with and encourage others who have suffered. I have shared the story of my brother's murder and the power of forgiveness to people in many nations, including Sudan, Indonesia, Egypt, and Libya. My suffering was insignificant compared to what most of them have experienced. Being able to sympathize with people in their losses serves as an incredible bridge to share Christ's love.

The difference between suffering with God's power or without God's power is great. Many people are suffering great atrocities at the hands of evil and corrupt people. Because they don't know Christ or His power in their lives, they become crippled in bitterness, which has caused physical sickness in their bodies as well. Many continue to live in physical, emotional and spiritual bondage when Christ wants to take them through their pain to the other side of the redemption in their loss.

In August 2006, I went on a mission trip to northern Sudan. We spent time doing ministry and outreach in the refugee camps outside of Khartoum.

The refugees in these camps were displaced from southern Sudan and the Darfur area. Many of the residents had been there for years, living in huts made of cardboard boxes, newspaper and trash bags — the most extreme poverty I had ever seen. Most suffered from post-traumatic stress disorder and other disorders because of the traumatic abuse and violence they had endured. I had the opportunity to minister God's healing touch into the hearts of many women who needed to know they have a savior who died for the sins committed against them, and who could identify with their suffering. We were able to see them experience freedom from bitterness as they transferred the wrongs committed against them up to heaven's courtroom. In addition, we were able to call forth the emerging generation of youth to bring reconciliation to their nation on behalf of the wrongs committed against their parents' generation.

Sudan has a long history of ethic and religious strife between Arabs, black Africans, Christians and Muslims. Even before the crises in Darfur, there was mass genocide of Christians in southern Sudan. Refugees from the south were forced from their homes and fled to camps in the north. God is calling this generation of youth to embrace the ultimate act of redemptive suffering, which is to reach out and bridge the divide and love their enemies, whom they now live among in northern Sudan. If they embrace this call, I believe we could see a whole generation of northern Sudanese people, most of whom are Muslim, receiving the redeeming power of Jesus Christ.

Just as God is calling forth a generation of Sudanese refugees to use personal reconciliation to be a bridge to reconcile a nation of unbelievers to Christ, He is calling me to do the same in Libya.

Chapter 13 — In Search Of Reconciliation

"Mercy and truth are met together; righteousness and peace have kissed each other."
— *Psalm 85:10 KJV*

After Abdel Basset El Megrahi was convicted and sentenced for the Lockerbie bombing, a civil lawsuit was filed against the Libyan government. Since Megrahi was a Libyan intelligence agent, there was an assumption that he was acting under the authority of the Libyan government. The civil lawsuit resulted in a structured settlement agreement that had very specific requirements that would incrementally move Libya and the United States toward reconciliation and fully normalized relations.

The first requirement was the admission of responsibility by the Libyan government for the actions of an intelligence agent of their county. In its carefully crafted acceptance of responsibility, Libya did not admit it was responsible, but rather said that because Megrahi was convicted, the nation would accept responsibility. All along, Libya has continued to say it had nothing to do with the bombing.

The settlement agreement provided for punitive damages against the government that are higher than compensatory damages and designed to punish the responsible party and deter future behavior. An agreement was made that Libya would pay $10 million per victim to each of their families. The payments were to be made in three separate intervals with requirements tied to each payment. It was a complex process that was directly tied to involvement of the U.S. and Libyan governments. Although the U.S. government was not a direct party to the lawsuit, complex political issues became intertwined as requirements in the suit.

The U.N. sanctions were lifted September 12, 2003, after Libya accepted responsibility. The Libyan government made good on paying the first two settlement payments and on December 19, 2003, agreed to dismantle its weapons of mass destruction as was required. In February 2004, travel restrictions to Libya were lifted. In June 2004, the U.S. opened a liaison office in Tripoli — an office that doesn't have full embassy status but serves as a liaison between the two countries. A month later, Libya opened a liaison office in Washington, D.C.

President Bush lifted the U.S. sanctions on Libya in September 2004. And finally in May 2006, Libya was removed from the U.S. list of state sponsors of terrorism — a place Libya had held since 1979.

Things seemed to progressing along nicely between the two nations until there was an allegation that Muammar Gaddafi had ordered a "hit" on the president of Saudi Arabia. Because of the U.S. government's strong relationship with the Saudi president, this allegation stalled the progress that was being made.

As a result, the escrow payment that the Libyans had made of the final payment lapsed. If that wasn't enough, several Bulgarian nurses and a Palestinian doctor were arrested for allegedly infecting hundreds of Libyan children with HIV/AIDS during the 1990s. Their resulting conviction brought a cry of outrage from the world community on what they saw as a kangaroo court and a conviction based on incredible evidence. The moral outrage of the world community on this issue put it on a list of unrelated items that the U.S. government demanded be resolved before full normalized relations would be restored.

I was happy when the Libyan government took responsibility for the bombing and agreed to a fair settlement with the victims' families. Their behavior indicated a true commitment to reconciliation. Of course, money will never replace my brother Ken. If given the choice, my family would much rather have Ken back. As a lawyer, I know that a stiff civil judgment against someone can have the same effect as a criminal conviction.

In the case of state-sponsored terrorism that was alleged against Libya, it would be next to impossible to find enough evidence to convict President Gaddafi directly. The next option is to require payment of damages or restitution to the families in an effort to move them toward restoration. The Scriptures clearly require payment of restitution as a requirement of making the wrong right. (See Numbers 5:7-8 and Exodus 22:3-14) Payment of restitution shows a true heart change and commitment to move toward reconciliation. Without restitution, true reconciliation is impossible.

Personal Path To Reconciliation

While the quest for reconciliation between the United States and Libya was ongoing, the Lord was taking me on my own journey to reconciliation. I started to look at the verses in the Bible on reconciliation in a completely new way. Colossians 1:19-23 NLT says, "For God in all his fullness was pleased to live in Christ, and by him God reconciled everything in heaven and on earth by means of his blood on the cross. This included you who were once so far away from God. You were his enemies, separated from him by your evil thoughts and action, yet now, He has brought you back as His friends. He has done this through His death on the cross in His human body." In the past, I saw this Scripture in relation to God's redemptive purposes for me. But God began to broaden my perspective on the application of this passage to the redemptive purposes He wanted to see come out of my brother Ken's death. God began to show me that just as Christ performed the ultimate act of love and sacrifice and died on the cross while I was still His enemy, He was asking me to do the same. Just as Christ had died to reconcile people to Himself and bring them peace, He was asking believers to do the same in order to reconcile people to Christ, who is the true source of peace.

Grace is at the heart of reconciliation. "It is the silent partner but the strongest member in the spirituality of reconciliation. It prompts truth, allows for mercy, ensures justice and delivers peace."[xxii] He was asking me to die to my selfish desire to withhold love and extend the branch of peace to the Libyan government and its people.

In many ways, my response as a follower of Christ was very different than the response of nonbelievers. To most, reaching out and extending the hand to pursue love and reconciliation looks like foolishness, especially with a country like Libya that only took responsibility half-way. I wasn't the only Lockerbie family member who has responded this way. Reverend John Mosey and his wife Lisa, of England lost their 19-year-old daughter, Helga on Pan Am Flight 103. We have become good friends as we have shared our common desire to see our family members' deaths redeemed by seeing God glorified in the midst of it. The Moseys, too, had a deep desire from the very beginning to respond in a way of forgiveness toward the Libyan government and to extend the hand of love to the Libyan people. One reporter who featured Reverend Mosey's story and his heart toward the Libyans referred to it as the "insanity of grace." It was a fitting description, because it illustrated the way our actions were perceived by worldly terms.

During the trial itself, Reverend Mosey befriended a Libyan diplomat. Years later, after the trial, that same Libyan official invited Mosey as a guest to Libya. He visited several facilities in Libya, looking for a way to serve. He ended up purchasing an ambulance for a home for special needs children and having it shipped to Libya. It was given to Libya as a symbol of God's love for the people of Libya.

I will confess that I didn't really know what it looked like to walk out loving Libya in practical terms for my life. So I have had to stay in tune to the Holy Spirit and His direction in the process.

After the Libyan government opened a liaison office in Washington in 2004, Ali Aujali was appointed as the Libyan Ambassador. I sent a letter to him introducing myself and began the process of nurturing a relationship with him. In another letter, I shared with him that I was a Christian and that I needed to forgive the Libyan people for my brother's death and move toward reconciliation. In order to do that, I needed to be able to go to Libya and meet them so I could see them in a different light than I had seen them for the last 15 years. I asked his assistance in facilitating a trip for me to Libya, since it was still impossible to obtain a visa.

Prior to this, in late 2003, the Lord began to speak to me about doing a reconciliation confer-ence in Libya. I really had no idea how to make that happen, so I just continued to pray. In January 2004, I attended a conference where I became acquainted with a Congressional staffer who worked as the foreign relations advisor for a Congressman who was a member of one of the international relations subcommittees. He also had a strong faith in Christ and is daily involved in building bridges of friendship with leaders from around the world. Unbeknownst to me, this Congressman had been in discussion with Dr. Treki, the Libyan Ambassador to the United Nations, about holding such a conference in Libya. It was to be a private dialogue with about 20 leaders total, including select governmental officials and religious leaders from each country. The purpose was to dialogue on commonalities between Islam and Christianity, and I was invited to be a speaker. The timing of the conference was still to be determined based on funding and unresolved Lockerbie issues.

During 2004, I continued to keep in touch with Ambassador Aujali and asked if he would facilitate a meeting with Gaddafi when I went to Libya. I also began to explore other avenues of going to Libya. One day I was surfing the Internet, when I stumbled across a tour that was being planned to Libya in January 2005. Even if my first trip wasn't to involve official meetings with Libyan leaders, I knew I had to go. Upon being accepted as a part of the tour, I sent the details of it to Ambassador Aujali and asked if he could arrange a meeting with Gaddafi. Aujali assured me he would do his best.

On the day we left for Libya, there were still no confirmed meetings. In fact, when we arrived at London Heathrow Airport, we still did not have our visas. Then without any clue how we obtained them, we were on our way. I found out later Ambassador Aujali helped us get the visas.

Our tour was set to last 12 days, and my friend, Lisa Flake and I were planning to stay an extra three days. My assignment from the Lord was clear. I was to meet with individuals and governmental officials. I was to tell them my story — I was the first American Lockerbie relative to go to Libya — and share that as a follower of Christ, I needed to visit to Libya to get to know the people, forgive them, and learn to love them.

Libya is a beautiful country that is uncorrupted by the pushiness of the tourist industry that exists in other parts of the world. The historic sites of Greek, Roman and Byzantines, located along the Mediterranean Sea, are the most well preserved of any I had ever seen. The smell of fresh seawater permeated the air as we walked the ruins and prayed silently to ourselves. I could clearly imagine the bustling cities that once existed in these places. I was most intrigued by Cyrene, which was located in Eastern Libya in the region known as Cyrenaica. Cyrene was the birthplace of Simon of Cyrene, the man who helped Jesus carry the cross to Calvary. Many believed that after observing the miracles at Calvary, Simon went on to become the leader of the first church in North Africa.

At Cyrene, I was most fascinated by the early influences of Christian church that remained from the Byzantine Empire. There were remains of old churches with crosses and baptismals.

Our Muslim guide, Ali, demonstrated the way the baptism worked as he walked down one side of the baptismal into the imaginary water and out the other side declaring, "My sins are forgiven." I felt it was a prophetic picture of God's continued heart for that land and the Libyan people.

We talked with our guides and other friends we met along the way about U.S. and Libyan relations. Ali illustrated how he saw it with his body language, saying, "For many years Gaddafi has been facing the East and now he is facing the West, and this is very good." Ali believed that for years, Gaddafi had been aligning himself with the ways of the Middle East and now was aligning more with the ways of the West. Gaddafi has indeed shown signs of turning Libya from its former ways, particularly its involvement in terrorism. But whether Gaddafi has experienced a true heart change is hard to tell.

Everyone we met in Libya was friendly and welcoming. People were always careful to separate their view of U.S. foreign policy from their view of Americans. We felt like we were celebrities, because few of the Libyan people had ever met Americans.

When I shared my Lockerbie story with people, I received a mixed reaction. At first there was a bit of disbelief. I found that for years, they had been told that Lockerbie was a conspiracy by the United States government against their country. Now that they stood face to face with a victim, they did not know what to believe.

Some feared that my reasons for coming were to cause trouble or to make a big stink about the Lockerbie issue that they were all trying to forget. I could discern a deep sense of societal shame in the hearts of the Libyan people. They were a proud people, but deeply wounded by the world community viewing them all as terrorists.

As I assured them of my good intentions of being in Libya, people became more at ease. Ideas of forgiveness and loving your enemies are not generally Muslim concepts. Even Christians who are supposed to live by these teachings don't know what it looks like to love your enemies. But as I shared my story, time and again I would see the walls fall. Even grown Libyan men began to weep. One of our guides, Iyad, took me into his arms and said, "It is so good for you to come. I will do anything I can to help you."

During the trip, I honestly didn't know what to make of it all. Then God began to show me the reason we are called to love our enemies. It isn't just this noble idea in Scripture. God showed me that there is power in loving my enemies that breaks something in the spiritual realm. My simple act of obedience broke down the walls of pride and we were able to be transparent with each other. I was sharing the gospel with them in words and action. It was the most powerful experience of my life. For the first time, I understood the power of the gospel and how Christ came to us and loved us while we were yet enemies. I just got a taste of it and I knew I wanted more.

Then something began to shift in me. I found myself asking the Libyan people questions like "What was it like when the U.S. bombed Tripoli in 1986?" and "What is it like to live in Libya?" Time and again I received responses of shock. Another guide, Hamid, said, "No one has ever asked me that question. It is so good of you to ask." Fear of the secret police often keeps people from sharing their hearts. But many times, I had people pull me aside to more discreet locations so they could share about their lives in Libya. I could tell that it was really important for them to be able to share. It is human nature to want to be known. One man told me about how he had been educated in the United States years before U.S./Libya relations began to fall apart. He described America as his spiritual home. I have often pondered that statement and the meaning behind it. Although I will never know for sure what he meant by that statement, it was as if what he was not saying, was speaking louder than those few simple words that he uttered. My heart was softening. I found that the people I had once looked upon as enemies, were now my friends.

President Gaddafi declined to meet with me on that trip, but I did meet with the Secretary of Tourism and the Secretary of Planning. There had been some opposition to these meetings happening. But God spoke to my heart, "My purposes will not be frustrated." So in faith, after the Secretary of Tourism canceled our meeting, I asked our guide to take us to his office anyway. I only needed a few minutes to deliver my greeting and share why I came. It was a bit scary as a woman going into that exclusively male-dominated environment. I figured what was the worst they could do, but turn us away? Our guide was nervous about what would happen, but he agreed to take us because he believed in what we were doing. But the government officials were friendly and hospitable. After coffee and customary mint tea, we took photos and then went about our way.

After our meeting with the cabinet officials, it was unclear exactly what we accomplished. I felt peace that God's purposes had been fulfilled, even if I did not understand them. I knew one thing for sure, on that trip I gained a new-found love and respect for the Libyan people. I had just gotten a taste of God's redemptive heart for the Libyan people and I knew I wanted more.

As I continued to press into the Lord, God has showed me His deep longing for His lost children of Libya to be back in relationship with Him. I feel His heart for the Libyan people, and that compels me to reach out to them. Tears come quickly to my eyes when I think about this. It leaves my heart heavy, and all other concerns disappear. There is an agony in the heart of God to be reunited with His desperate and lost children. He sees His children walking around broken, wounded and confused. His all-consuming love compelled Him to take away the division. Ever since the garden and the fall, there has been a void in His heart as He has yearned to be back in intimate fellowship with His children. Dying for His children was the only way He could be reunited and reconciled to them and end the power of sin in their lives. Any loving parent would do the same for their children. They would sacrifice their finances or their own life and well-being in order to provide for their children and to see them healed and brought home.

God desires to cultivate in each of us the same burning love and compulsion to see His lost children reunited to Him. This is the burning passion and love that compels me to reach out to the Libyan people. I feel the ache of God's heart for them that I cannot remain silent or uninvolved. I am moved to tears as I think about a whole nation that doesn't know Jesus or His healing power.

As the Apostle Paul talked about being compelled by love into the ministry of reconciliation, I feel that same compulsion and want to challenge others to being involved as well.

Chapter 14 — Overcoming Evil With Good

"Do not be overcome by evil, but overcome evil with good." — Romans 12:21 NIV

In early 2006, plans were under way to hold a reconciliation conference in Libya. A foundation had committed to fund the appropriate travel expenses for four Congressmen to travel to Libya, but at the last minute the funds were pulled. I was very disappointed to hear the news, because I believed in my heart that the conference was supposed to happen. The postponement caused me to develop a much broader vision of how God wanted me to be involved in Libya.

During the Thanksgiving holiday in 2005, I drove home with my best friend Karen Martello, to celebrate with her and her family. It was a particularly emotional time for me as I was seeing a counselor and working through a lot of healing in my own heart. I was also sensing change was on the horizon for my life. I had been working for a mission organization for several years and felt God was preparing me to birth something new. God had begun to stir in my heart a vision to launch my own organization. I had always had an entrepreneurial spirit and was a visionary and strategist by nature, but I was unsure of what God wanted me to do.

The day after Thanksgiving, Karen and I headed into downtown Chicago to spend the day sightseeing. We wandered up and down Michigan Avenue and talked about life. Being an oral processor by nature, I don't always fully understand what I am thinking or feeling about things until they come out of my mouth. Karen served as a midwife in my process of birthing a new vision. As we walked and talked, I began to share a bit of my vision of starting an organization where we would attack the social evils of terrorism, oppression, injustice and poverty, to name a few. Karen said in a matter of fact way, "Why don't you just start your own foundation?"

It was the first time I had allowed myself to seriously consider the prospect. Always an advocate, my life had often been focused on using advocacy to be an agent of change. The previous fall, I had attended a class at Freedom Church in Colorado Springs taught by C. Peter Wagner called "The Church in the Workplace." Wagner is the founder of an apostolic ministry called Global Harvest Ministries that equips leaders in the church to complete the Great Commission, especially among the least reached areas of the world. Wagner taught on the principle that the gospel is designed not only to change the lives of individuals, but to transform society. It wasn't necessarily a new concept, but I was seeing it through new eyes. I realized that I could use advocacy to persuade leaders of nations to change the way they did business, or I could be a part of imparting the transformational power of Jesus Christ into the lives of the leaders. If leaders received the true life change that comes only through Jesus Christ, the results should affect the way they rule, which would trickle down in fair policies to the people they serve.

I was excited about the prospect of launching my own organization, but I was unsure of the need. Our vision was to start a foundation that could fund bridge-building events like the reconciliation conference we were planning to do in Libya. Who better to seek advice from than members of Congress that have a real vision for building bridges of friendship with leaders from other nations. So Karen and I scheduled a meeting with some Congressional leaders in late March 2006 in Washington, D.C. We also scheduled a meeting with Ambassador Aujali from Libya the same day.

We first went to the Libyan Embassy to meet with Ambassador Ali Aujali. We also met the Secretary of Housing for Libya, who was in town visiting. He offered his kind condolences for my loss and assured me that Libya was not responsible for the Lockerbie bombing. I asked about the U.S. bombing of Tripoli in 1986 and he showed me a scar on his forehead where he was injured from falling debris during the air strike. I shared with them about my trip to Libya and how I wanted to find some way to serve in Libya. Both men kindly offered to assist me in any way possible. After ending the meeting with a nice lunch with Ambassador Aujali and his deputy director, Karen and I rushed off to make our next appointment on Capital Hill.

Members of Congress could not have been more supportive of our idea to start an organization to fund and facilitate similar dialogues to what had been planned for the reconciliation conference in Libya. In fact, a group of members of Congress had initiated a bipartisan group to encourage individuals and organizations in the United States to build bridges for people-to-people diplomacy, humanitarian service, and cultural and educational exchanges. There was a recognition that people in the U.S. and other Western nations have been blessed much more and have much to offer to the developing world, just as we have much to learn from them.

One Congressman urged us, "Just pick a country and start!"

"How about Libya?" I said.

Could it be that simple, I thought to myself. I knew I still had much work ahead of me. I had to get the buy-in of the Libyan government and handle the incorporation process of our new organization. But I had never felt a greater sense of peace with what I was called to do.

The Call Is Confirmed

As I continued to pray about starting this organization, I was amazed by the divine favor I felt. I have heard it said that God gives people extra grace when He is directing you into a higher call or requiring increased measures of faith. There were a few moments when I found myself questioning why God had called me to do this. A woman seeking to pioneer in a Muslim country would be seen as foolishness in the world's eyes. But God made it clear that this was His deal and not mine, so I didn't have to fear.

So often in the church, women who are called into leadership are looked down upon. I have had more than one well-meaning man in the church say that the reason God was using me in a leadership role was because He had called a man to do it, but he abdicated. Some more radically viewed people have even accused me of downright disobedience in serving in leadership in ministry. At times, Christian women struggle with being faithful to the calls on our lives. I recognized the magnitude of what God was calling me to. I wanted to make absolutely sure it was really His will. So I asked Him why He hadn't called a man to do it. His words pierced deep within my heart. "I chose you because you are a woman. I need someone who has a deep love for the Libyan people and a genuine heart to serve them. Because you are a woman, they won't feel threatened by you."

In June 2006, I was already actively at work filling out the incorporation paperwork and preparing to launch the organization. I was invited by some friends to spend a couple days taking a course on the end times at the International House of Prayer (IHOP) in Kansas City. I had heard many stories about the powerful presence of God at IHOP and hoped I would have some quality time just soaking up God's presence while I was there. Before leaving for IHOP, I had been praying about the magnitude of the call on my life and really felt burdened with the task. One night I felt led to pray, "Lord, if I am going to do this thing, I need to get my marching orders directly from You. I need to be in Your throne room." It seemed like a bold request, but I had heard of other people asking God for such things. Even Moses understood the magnitude of the task he was called to in leading the children of Israel. In Exodus 33:12-14 NLT "Moses said to the Lord, 'You have been telling me, "Take these people up to the Promised Land." But you haven't told me whom you will send with me. You call me by name and tell me I have found favor with you. Please, if this is really so, show me your intentions so I will understand you more fully and do exactly what you want me to do. Besides don't forget that this nation is your very own people.'" God honored his request and even allowed Moses to see His glory, all because God considered Moses His friend and he had found favor with Him.

During a break from our class at IHOP, our group went to spend some time soaking in the presence of God at the prayer room. During worship, the prayer leader asked people taking the Omega class, the course on the end times, to stand up so others could come over and pray for us. Four prayer leaders came over and laid hands on me as I closed my eyes. One woman began to pray that God knew my desire to come up to His throne room. As she prayed, I had an open vision of me as a child floating up through the sky into the heavens. It was the most amazing spiritual experience of my life. The spiritual climate of heaven was all about love. It was as if the feeling of love was just whirling about me. Jesus spoke to me directly about the call He had placed on my life and showed me the sphere of my authority through the clouds. I could clearly see North Africa and parts of the Middle East. His words were clear: My call was to love the leaders of North Africa and the Middle East. It seemed so simple, but also so profound. He was speaking this call to me as a little child. I felt scared by the depth of the call. I promised to do it, just as long as Jesus didn't let go of my hand. He promised that He would not let me go. To this day, I am still hanging on tight.

For the first time in my life, I felt a deep sense of affirmation from the Lord in what He was calling me to. He assured me that He's using me because I have an authentic voice on terrorism and what it means to walk out the redemptive purposes of such a tragedy. Just like Deborah, who led the troops into victory against Sisera's army and gave God all the glory in Judges 5, God was expecting the same of me. Unlike Deborah, I wasn't called into a physical battle, but rather into a spiritual battle armed with the weapon of genuine heartfelt love. But like Deborah, I would be foolish to do this if it was anything less than God's call.

Peace And Prosperity
As I have traveled around the world, the two things I see time and again that people want are peace

and prosperity. But prosperity is much broader than financial blessing. Prosperity is about success and well-being. As believers, we know that true peace and prosperity only comes from Jesus Christ. We named the organization the Peace and Prosperity Alliance because we exist to share our peace and prosperity with other nations.

The words *peace* and *prosperity* can be found in countless places in the Bible. The scripture God gave me as the foundational scripture for the alliance is Zechariah 3:8-10 NLT. It says, "Soon, I am going to bring my servant the Branch...and I will remove the sins of this land in a single day. And on that day, says the Lord Almighty, each of you will invite your neighbor into your home to share your peace and prosperity."

We extend the branch of peace by building bridges of friendship between leaders and helping them serve other leaders in the developing world through education, training and humanitarian assistance.

Waging War With Love

The Peace and Prosperity Alliance has become the main conduit for my walking out Romans 12:20-21 NLT. It says, "If your enemies are hungry feed them. If they are thirsty, give them something to drink. In doing this, you will heap burning coals of shame on their heads. Don't let evil conquer you, but conquer evil by doing good." We are truly in a battle. Too often, the church falls victim to engaging in the spiritual battle we are in by using the enemy's weapons. Like any great military strategy, we need to fully understand the enemy's strategies in order to counter them. But in order to win the battle that we are waging against the enemy, we must walk in the opposite spirit. On more than one occasion, I have heard Christians expressing words of hate or fear towards Muslims. That is the weapon the enemy would expect. But by responding in the opposite spirit, it takes the enemy by surprise. Where there is hate, we must respond in love. If we are hit with fear, we must respond in faith. In deception, we respond with truth. Christ won the battle in the most unlikely way — by dying. In addition, Scripture tells us that we overcome the enemy by the blood of the lamb and the word of our testimony. The blood of the lamb brings forgiveness, and the word of the testimony is the redemptive truth of God's restorative power in our lives. Those who have been most hurt by wrong- doing are the ones most equipped to win the battle against their offender. They are not battling their offender, however, but rather the enemy at work in the person who hurt them.

When Christians try to battle with the enemy's weapons, they end up ineffective. If they aren't able to see the redemptive power in forgiveness, doing good to their enemy and sharing their redemptive testimony, they miss out on an opportunity to see God glorified in their loss.

Since my brother's death, I have always wanted to see some kind of good come out of it. We are starting to see that desire become a reality through the Peace and Prosperity Alliance. In September 2007, we held a charity golf scramble in Colorado Springs, Colorado in cooperation with the Libyan Embassy, to benefit children in Libya with HIV/AIDS. Ambassador Ali Aujali participated in the event and I had the privilege of playing golf with him. The event raised $25,000 to benefit those children in need.

God continues to open doors to serve in Libya. The Libyan government and the Gaddafi Development Foundation, an international non-governmental organization that carries out humanitarian activities in the social, economic, cultural and human rights fields, have asked the alliance to facilitate projects in Libya. These projects include training for English teachers, medical training and medical procedures, and to host symbolic reconciliation trips in which Americans can go to Libya to learn about their culture and lives and help move our countries toward full reconciliation.

Justice And Mercy

For nearly 20 years, I have fought hard for justice. The Lockerbie tragedy has affected nearly every part of my life, including my decision to become a lawyer, a child advocate, to get involved in missions and to start the Peace and Prosperity Alliance. Seeing justice done has always been important for me. After a successful criminal conviction, civil judgment and admission of responsibility by Libya's leaders, new evidence threatens to throw the case wide open again and could alter the judgment in the Lockerbie case. With an appeal pending, I find myself questioning whether we will ever see true justice in this lifetime.

We serve a just God. He has put within each of us an inner conviction to see justice achieved for the abused, oppressed and downtrodden. But many of us will never see true justice in our lifetime. Instead, justice will only come when our case is litigated in heaven's courtroom. Then, the Lord, who has made Himself the advocate, judge and the jury, will surely bring justice and right the wrong.

While I wait until glory to see true justice served, I will pursue the road less traveled. I will extend the ultimate act of sacrifice and mercy by reaching out with the love of Jesus Christ, believing that God will use it to draw people to Himself. Taking hate and turning it around with love is the only way to make my brother's death not be in vain.

Contact information

Lisa Gibson is the Founder and Executive Director of the Peace and Prosperity Alliance. The Peace and Prosperity Alliance is a 501c3 charity that exists to bridge the gap between the developed and developing world through cross-cultural partnerships between government, business, civic and religious leaders that will result in lasting change. You may contact her through:

Peace and Prosperity Alliance
4252 Beautiful Circle
Castle Rock, CO
info@peaceandprosperityalliance.org

To obtain a **free copy** of a bonus teaching CD or to book Lisa for a speaking engagement, please contact us at: info@peaceandprosperityalliance.org or visit us at www.peaceandprosperityalliance.org.

Endnotes:

[i]Keith Swartley, "Qur'an, Hadith, And Shari'a," *Encountering the World of Islam,* Lesson 3, (Authentic Media, 2005), p. 83.

[ii]Ibid.

[iii]Ibid.

[iv]Ibid, p. 85.

[v]C. George Fry and James R. King, "Islamic Religious Practices: The Pillars of Faith," *Encountering the World of Islam,* Lesson 3, (Authentic Media, 2005), p.88.

[vi]Ibid, p. 90.

[vii]Ibid, p. 94.

viii Ibid, p. 92.

ix Ibid, p. 95-96.

x Ibid, p. 98.

xi Ibid, p. 99.

xii Ibid.

xiii Phil Parshall, "Diversity Within Muslim Umma," *Encountering the World of Islam*, Lesson 4, (Authentic Media, 2005), p. 123.

xiv Ibid, p. 123.

xv Ibid, p. 124.

xvi Jay Tolson, "Caliph Wanted: Why An Old Islamic Institution Resonates With Many Muslims Today," *US News and World Report*, (January 14, 2008), p. 38.

xvii Ibid, p. 38.

xviii Ibid.

xix Joel Richardson, "Antichrist Islam's Awaited Messiah," (Pleasant Word, 2006), p.43

[xx]George Lardner, Jr., "2 Libyans Indicted in Pan Am Blast," Washington Post, November 15, 1991; page A01.

[xxi]Ibid.

[xxii]Robert A. Seiple, "Ambassadors of Hope", (Intervarsity Press, 2004), p.84.

Printed in the United States
125431LV00001B/2/P